Monoskiing

Monoskiing

MARTYN HURN

The Crowood Press

First published in 1988 by
The Crowood Press
Ramsbury, Marlborough,
Wiltshire SN8 2HE

British Library Cataloguing in Publication Data

Hurn, Martyn
  Monoskiing.
  1. Skiing – Manuals
  I. Title
  796.93

  ISBN 1 85223 158 0

Typeset by Chippendale Type, Otley, West Yorkshire
Printed in Great Britain at the University Printing House, Oxford

For Clare

Contents

Acknowledgements

The first acknowledgement in a book of this nature must go to the many patient students from whose feedback the ideas have evolved, but my greatest thanks must go to Liz Colthurst without whose help and untiring good humour I could not have written the book. Thirdly I must thank David Goldsmith for providing me with material from which I was able to write about the history of monoskiing, Denise Nicholls for her superb diagrams, and, last but not least, Europa Sport and Phoenix Mountaineering Ltd for their help in providing me with the necessary equipment.

Preface

Since the early days when men first used skis to travel around the snowy kingdoms there were those amongst them who enjoyed these tools for sport; men and women who fed on the thrill of flying down ever steeper slopes upon their skis, not to get from one village to the next, but just for fun. One of the most daring of them was a young man called Hans. There was not a slope or mountain that would not yield to his skill.

One day an old man visited the village where Hans lived. The village folk were celebrating Han's descent of the North Face of Mt Kracksen, a very steep and treacherous slope visible high above the village.

'What is everybody rejoicing over?' asked the old man. When he was told, he was unimpressed.

'I have seen a man ski a slope far steeper and of ten times the length,' he retorted. The villagers thought the old man was mad; after all, everybody knew that Hans was the best skier in the region and many believed, in the whole world. Later that night word of the old man's comment reached Hans, who, despite his fame, was a humble man. Intrigued, he decided to find out more.

'The man you seek lives in a far-off region of the mountains. Travel with caution, for there will be many hazards – but also many revelations if you look with truly open eyes.'

Hans set off immediately – the tales of his long journey are legendary – but eventually he arrived in a high mountain valley fitting the description the old man had given him. Hans looked around him. Never before had he seen such slopes, such huge precipitous peaks. Even in his wildest dreams he could not see himself skiing these slopes. 'Where could a man ski?' he kept asking himself.

He found a good vantage point and waited in the hope that he might see this mystical skier. After several days he had seen no one and began to doubt the old man's description – but then he saw him. High above some ice cliffs, swooping down the slope, he came right to the edge of the cliffs, the spray from his turns cascading down. His speed was amazing, yet he skied like no man Hans had seen before; his turns were strange and his manoeuvres beyond Han's imagination. He watched for many days, trying to learn and absorb what was happening, trying to muster enough courage to attempt the same slopes.

No one knew if he found the courage; nor did they ask, such was their respect for him. They did, however, question him about the man he spent so long searching for.

'How did he ski?'

'What could he ski?'

'How good was he?'

His eyes distant, as though recalling something half real, half dreamt, Hans would reply, 'Anything – he could ski anything. He was the best, the best there is, and his turns were so fluid it was as though he were only on one ski.'

Introduction

When I wrote about monoskiing in *Skiing Real Snow* I was very conscious of the fact that monoskiing had a very different atmosphere. It seemed to reach beyond the confines of two skis and allow the skiers to take a fresh look at the terrain in which they were skiing. It was my feeling then, and now, that those teaching monoskiing should refrain from getting too engrossed in its technicalities but rather concentrate upon encouraging individual styles and manoeuvres to develop, providing that the student can move around the terrain in reasonable comfort and with confidence.

The mono is basically quite an easy machine to use and it is within the capabilities of most intermediate skiers and above. As long as you can do rough parallels you should be able to get some fun out of the mono, and this is the crux of my teaching method. I do not aim to produce perfect copies of the perfect skiing machine (whoever that may be), but rather to let the criteria for optimum performance be to get down without injuring yourself and to have the best time of your life! The mono ski can open many doors for you – it will take you into terrain you may not have visited before, it will probably change the way in which you look at snow slopes, and it will offer a number of new and exciting manoeuvres. I have suggested a few different styles in the hope that you will be able to adopt one (or a variation of it) to suit your needs, which you can then incorporate into your own style.

In the following pages you will not find an in-depth breakdown of the technique of monoskiing but rather a progressive series of suggestions that you could try. I believe that we learn by experimenting; the instructor can only offer guidelines within which you should operate. By finding out what works for you within these guidelines you will gradually acquire the skill you desire (experiment by leaning a little more or bending part of your body more until the desired effect is obtained).

The mono ski will allow you to go into terrain that may well be unfamiliar to you, particularly the off-piste where the mono performs best. This terrain has many hazards that you do not find on-piste and it would be irresponsible of me to encourage you into it without making you aware of its dangers.

I hope that these pages will give you a good grounding in the art of monoskiing and that they will excite you to experiment further and in so doing take your skiing into new realms of performance.

Author's Note

If you have not read *Skiing Real Snow*, I suggest that you read Appendix 2 on learning techniques before you reach the slopes, as it will help you to get the most from the text and diagrams. Readers of *Skiing Real Snow* should not assume that the techniques are identical, as each diagram has been carefully redrawn to include the subtle differences between the techniques used on a mono and those on two skis. Furthermore, if you have little or no experience of off-piste skiing and its intrinsic dangers, you would also be well advised to read Appendix 1, Avalanche Awareness, before going out on to the snow.

1 History and Equipment

Back in the mid 1970s an American surf champion turned skier called Mike Doyle had a vision of a new skiing vehicle, an idea born of his knowledge of the water and his enthusiasm for his new sport of skiing:

'I visualised a single ski because I know that one water ski works better than two. Powder snow is a lot like water and so I began thinking how one ski would work. I made my own at home, the first ones out of plywood and fibreglass – really crude – and they seemed to work. So I thought that if I could design it a little better, and put some edges on to it you would have something that would really work.'

After many changes and refinements a ski was finally commercially produced in 1978 by a Californian company called Bahne. The mono was 195cm long and was made of an aluminium honeycomb core wrapped in fibreglass. It was wider than two skis so that it could accommodate the width of the boots and its flex pattern and design was that of a classic powder ski with a soft broad tip to give it lift in the deep snow. The only other monos at that time were single skis with a high platform that allowed you to clamp both boots to it, but the Doyle design had the tremendous advantage that the boots were mounted straight on to the ski making it much more stable.

Doyle designed the ski specifically for off-piste skiing, but its potential in other terrain was realised even in the early days of its development:

'I designed it for powder, cruddy snow and the kind of snow that sucks up at the sole. But a lot of people are riding it in the moguls.

I've seen a lot of guys just flying through the bumps and really skiing the heck out of it.'

It was in the terrain away from the piste, however, that the mono really shone. It opened up a whole new range of man-oeuvres with names like upsidedowners and off-the-lips, terms usually associated with surfing. To quote Doyle again:

'If you're a surfer you look at the terrain totally differently from a skier. You start looking at the side walls and the lips and how to get your legs higher than your head when you're coming off the wall. Skiers always look at a nice bowl and look straight down that centre groove and ski figures of eight. I can see competition with the single ski but not in the present form of competition. I would set up more of a moto-cross course where you put the flags on the side of the hill, a flag down the bottom of a gully, a flag over a jump, another back down in a gully, I'd set up this interesting pattern. Skiers don't think that way at all – they think straight down the fall-line and they put flags all in a row.'

A little condescending perhaps, but now, ten years on, competitions are taking place in many shapes and forms and the mono is a common sight both off-piste and on-piste.

The mono began to be featured in the media and in the ski movies, starting with the films of Dick Barrymore and later the spectacular sequences of the *Apocalypse* film team in Les Arcs. Often at the forefront of skiing innovations, Les Arcs virtually adopted the mono as their own for a few years and it featured in their ski schools' teaching programme before many other resorts had even seen one.

13

After the first Bahne ski many other designs were tried, but few seemed to improve upon the original. In fact many who skied it in the late–1970s claim it is still the best mono around. The French firm of Duret took on most of the production of the boards in Europe, manufacturing a range of sizes and designs until the mid-1980s when many others, seeing the growing market, also produced boards. Some of these were excellent, others were likened to fish out of water or even more colourful images!

Choosing Your Mono

Not only did the functional designs of the mono change, but customised boards with beautiful airbrush designs were also introduced. When you go into a ski shop now, you are confronted with almost as many different designs of mono ski as you are of normal skis. So what criteria do you use to choose the right ski? First let us look at some of the design features and examine their various applications. As with so much modern technology it is changing by the minute and as I write this I am sure other innovations are coming off the drawing board, nevertheless certain criteria must remain constant.

Flex Pattern

The flex pattern of the mono will depend upon its internal construction and its external design. As with normal skis the softer flexing skis are more suited to the off-piste conditions of deep snow, whereas the stiffer designs work well on-piste and on harder snow. You will come across two basic external design features that help to soften the flex pattern: the swallow-tail and the split fore-ski. The former is simply a V-slot cut out of the tail, and the latter is a slit up the middle of the front of the ski bound by two holes to prevent it splitting the ski still further. Both these designs appear to work, but my own preference is for a ski in which

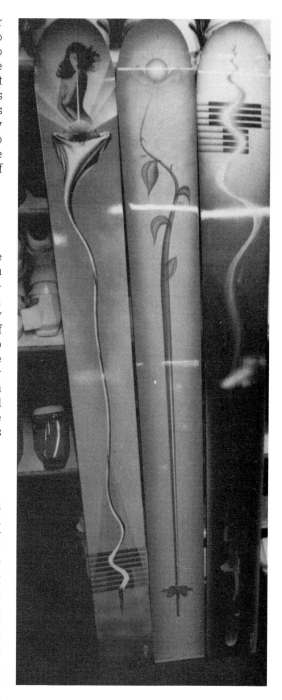

Fig 1 Beautiful airbrush designs.

14

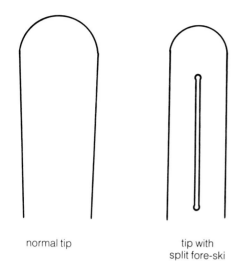

normal tip | tip with split fore-ski

Fig 2   Sometimes the tip of the ski is split to create a softer flexing edge.

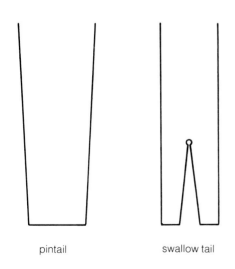

pintail | swallow tail

Fig 3   A similar effect is achieved on the tail of the ski by making a V-cut; this is usually known as a swallow-tail.

the flex pattern is controlled by its internal construction and, being a devotee of off-piste skiing, I favour the softer flex patterns.

If like me you want to use the ski mainly off-piste then make sure it also has a substantial shovel (the tip of the ski) as you will come across some models that have been designed for the piste or for racing – and these have minimal shovels.

Side-Cut

Next we must consider the side-cut (or lack of it) of the ski. After the original Bahne ski, many manufacturers produced skis that had no side-cut but which tapered towards the tail. These seemed to work all right off-piste (though no better than the Bahne) but were quite awkward on-piste. Many of the newer boards do have a side-cut; this is a more versatile design, and I would therefore recommend it.

Length

Finally, we must consider the length of the ski. A small ski used to be fashionable, but now long skis are thankfully back in favour. With improved construction the longer ski can be skied as easily as the shorter varieties and offer more stability. For beginners I would recommend a ski which is nearly as long as you are tall, and then, once you have mastered the basics, you can choose a longer model. Some may disagree, but I do not believe that the length of the mono is quite as critical as it is for normal skis. As the skis become more sophisticated, however, this may change.

You would probably be unwise to go out and purchase a mono straight away. Try as many different models as you can from the hire companies and settle on one which feels comfortable to ski in the conditions you are most likely to encounter.

Maintaining Your Mono

The mono should be treated just as normal skis when it comes to maintenance. The sole should be checked for holes and these should be filled with P-tex at the first opportunity to prevent water getting between the sole material and the ski, where it can freeze and expand, delaminating the sole in the process.

The edges should be kept sharp, although just as with normal skis, you should dull the edges at the tip and the tail of the ski. The amount can only be found by trial and error, but about ten to fifteen centimetres from either end will be a good starting point. If the ski continues to hook into the turns, dull the tip of the ski even further and if the ski seems to be grabbing at the back then increase the length of the dulling here as well. Be careful not to overdo it, however, because if the ski is not gripping on hard surfaces then these areas may need resharpening. Keeping the ski sole flat will be difficult, but as long as the edges are not railed then you need not worry unduly about the rest of the sole.

The sole will need waxing as normal, but be sure to use only a plastic scraper to remove excess wax as the edges of a metal one may catch and dig into the sole.

As with normal skis a mono will perform better, be easier to ski, and will last longer if it is well maintained.

Bindings

The bindings used on a mono ski are exactly the same as those used on normal skis, though they do have slight adaptations to the ski-brakes. Bindings vary in design because different manufacturers claim that different types of fall are more common than others. Some, for example, will say that most injuries result from a forward-twisting fall whilst others state that a backward-twisting fall is more hazardous; from their research they produce a binding that releases in a particular way, favouring one or other of the many ways in which you can fall over. The more you pay for a binding the more likely it is to cope with various types of fall. The manufacturers, of course, also build in other functions to try to sell their product.

Ease of use is important as you will frequently be skiing in deep snow, where it is often difficult to re-attach your ski.

Elasticity is almost as important as the release mechanism itself. When you ski – whether on one ski or two – you constantly rotate your feet, lift your heels and generally cause actions that tend to release the binding. The harder you ski, the greater these forces become. So how can the binding distinguish between a fall and just aggressive skiing? It does so by having built-in elasticity, which allows the foot to partly release under a certain pressure and then recentres the boot. If the pressure goes beyond that point, the binding will release, thus avoiding injury. This elasticity works best in the mid-range of the binding's settings and it therefore follows that you should ski with a binding that corresponds to your skiing ability and size. I will expand upon this idea later.

You should buy the best binding you can, though it would be difficult to distinguish between the best models of the major manufacturers. Whichever binding you choose it is vital that you adjust it properly. Contrary to popular belief, hire companies and shops often do not adjust the binding to your individual needs because they are not insured to do so – nor, in fact, is your instructor. So it therefore falls to you.

Adjusting Your Bindings

Fortunately, the most difficult adjustment, known as the pre-tension, is normally done by the shop. This setting allows the binding to accommodate the flexing of the ski and is adjusted when the boot is fitted to the binding. The other adjustments are all related to what is known as the DIN setting.

Binding Adjustment Chart

Weight (lb) (normal wt = height in cm − 100)	Release Setting Z min − max	Ability				Age	Boot Length mm	Release Setting Z
		Z	L	A	S			
109	3,6-4,6					<50 0		3·5
120	*3,9-5,0*	<2·5	−0·3	0	+0·3	51→60 -0·5	*270-310*	4
131	4,3-5,4	*2·5-5*	−0·5	0	*+0·5*	61→70 -1	280-320	4·5
142	4,6-5,9	>5	−1	0	+1	71→80 -1·5	280-320	*5*
153	5,0-6,3							5·5

Key: L – light speed
A – average speed
S – high speed
Boot length – if the actual boot length is different make the following correction; shorter = +0·5 Z
longer = −0·5 Z

Numbers in italics refer to the example for adusting your bindings, given below.

This is an internationally recognised scale of tensions that are the same for all bindings. There are two ways in which you can find out what your DIN setting is; from your weight and height, or from the size of your tibia head. These readings are then adjusted according to your age, skiing ability and length of boot sole. Let us look at a typical chart for a skier's weight (most of us do not have the facility to measure accurately the tibia head).

Let us assume that you are the correct weight for your height, and weigh about 120lb. This will give you a release, or DIN, setting (Z) of between 3.9 and 5.0. You now need to consult the ability column and decide which heading you come under. Let us flatter you and say that you ski at above average speed; you will therefore need to increase your release setting (Z) by 0.5 to 4.5 – 5.5 (rounding the figures up slightly). Next, your age must be taken into account if you are over 50 (youngsters may also need to make adjustments here; consult the manufacturer's recommendations).

Moving on, the size of your feet must be considered; let us assume your boot soles are only 270mm long, in which case they are less than the recommended figure for a release setting (Z) of 4.5. Therefore, 0.5 must be added, giving a final release setting (Z) or DIN number of between 5 and 6.

Every binding will operate through a range of DIN numbers and, as I said earlier, you should choose a binding in which your DIN number is in the middle of the range for that model. This will ensure that you gain the maximum benefit from the elasticity of the binding. More often than not the racing models that appear so attractive are not in fact suitable as their DIN number range is too high for most users.

Each manufacturer produces a table similar to the Binding Adjustment chart and you should always check it when setting your bindings. There are also a number of physical checks that you can carry out in the absence of such a chart.

The Toe-Unit

First, check the toe height. This is adjusted by rotating the screw at the top of the

17

binding – some newer models are adjusted by sliding the anti-friction pad to and fro. Unless the manufacturer advises otherwise, the height should be sufficient to allow a credit card to be slid between the boot sole and the pad when the boot is in position. The anti-friction pad should be checked for damage at the same time and be replaced if any is found – a simple job which can be done by most ski shops. The DIN number can be adjusted by a screw at the end of the binding and the setting read through a window on top. (Some models also require you to centre the boot by altering the wings of the unit, which is easily done.) Once you have adjusted it, see if you can twist the whole unit with your hand – your wrist strength is approximately the same as your ankle. If not, lighten the setting by 0.5 and try again. You should just be able to twist the toe-unit with your hand.

It is wise to carry out this check every time you put the ski on, as it will ensure that the binding has not frozen up or jammed.

The Heel-Unit

The heel-unit is adjusted by a screw at the rear of the binding and can be checked in the following way. Place the ski on the ground and put your right boot into the binding; step forward with the left foot and forcefully push the knee of your right leg towards the front of the ski, lifting the heel at the same time. It should take all your effort to release your foot in this way, but if it does release, you can be confident that it will in a fall. If it does not release with this action, lower the DIN number by 0.5 and try again. Some people need to practise the action and you may find that after a couple of attempts you can increase the setting slightly. Once one side has been checked repeat the procedure for the other side.

Maintaining bindings is straight forward and all I do is to slacken the units at the end of the season to save the springs. If they do require regreasing, be sure to use the grease recommended by the manufacturer as some are not suitable for the cold temperatures encountered when skiing.

Ski-Brakes or Leashes?

The problem with ski-brakes on mono skis is that they often do not work. Not only is it very inconvenient to walk a long way down to recover your ski but it could be very dangerous to any other skiers around, and in some resorts mono skiers must use leashes because of the unreliable performance of the brake. Fortunately most falls in deep snow, although spectacular because of the explosion of snow, do not involve you in the tumbling action that is a real danger with leashes. However, the quality of leashes is improving and there are some interesting designs available that all but prevent the possibility of a nasty bang on the head from a ski attached to you via a leash.

Finding Lost Skis

If you are not wearing leashes and fall off-piste, losing your ski in the process, the following advice may help you to relocate it. Mark the spot where you landed with a ski pole and start to search about two to three metres higher up the slope. It is important that you do not poke around aimlessly. Use your other pole or the tail of another ski and slice diagonally down the slope at about 50cm intervals and then repeat this in the other direction. The more you walk over the area the more likely you are to tread the lost ski deeper into the snow.

By being methodical in my searching I have never lost a ski and usually manage to find it quite quickly. If this search has not relocated it, check below you for signs that it has continued downwards. If a track is clear the ski will probably be easy to find at its end, but prepare yourself for a tiring walk, especially if the snow is deep.

Ski Poles

It is generally recommended that you ski with slightly longer than average poles when monoskiing as they are invaluable in helping your balance and because you will tend to adopt a higher stance than normal. However, I see no point in going out to buy specialist monoskiing poles unless you are really hooked, since normal poles will certainly suffice.

Boots

The boots used for monoskiing are exactly the same as for normal skiing and it is, of course, essential to choose the right ones. Many of you reading this book will be at the stage in your skiing where you might be considering buying a pair, so let me expand a little on the criteria to consider.

There are two basic types on the market, front entry and rear entry. Basically, the rear entry boot presents a smoother profile to the forefoot than the front entry type, but it is not as adjustable, so, if your foot fits easily, you will probably find these the most comfortable. If, however, you have an awkward foot then you may be better off with a front entry model. Rear entry boots are constantly changing and improving in their adjustability and by now probably have the greater share of the market.

Innovations in design occur every season and anything I might write about them here would probably be out of date in a matter of months. There are, however, a number of basic principles of which you ought to be aware and which apply to both front and rear entry models. Let us start by considering the flex pattern of the boot. When you look at the skiing techniques used in monoskiing you will see that, as for normal skiing, it is vital that you can flex your ankles. This will make your skiing more responsive, better balanced and more dynamic. Stiff ankles resulting from the skier buying the latest super-stiff racing boot are a major problem. These boots are usually your pride and joy, but all your instructor will want is to get rid of them. Fortunately, many of them now have adjustable forward flex – well worth looking for when choosing boots. You should only have this flex in the forward plane, as in all other directions it needs to be stiff. (A boot with a high stiff back is particularly useful for a technique used in monoskiing called straight-lining.) You should also be aware that when you test a boot in a shop the plastic will be supple because of the heat, and that when you get out on to the slope the boot will suddenly feel much stiffer – a good reason for having an adjustable flex system.

Be careful not to confuse this adjustable flex with adjustable forward lean. The latter only alters the angle at which the ankle is flexed; it is quite important, and you will have to experiment to see which position you find most comfortable. On a mono I prefer a more upright stance and so use less forward lean, but you should choose what you are happiest with.

Comfort should be your top priority when choosing boots. Without that you will never ski well, regardless of the number of gadgets and adjustments they have. Bearing this in mind, let me give you a few tips about finding a comfortable boot.

The boot should feel firm around the whole of the foot although you must be able to wriggle your toes around to prevent them getting cold. Be sure to push your shin bone against the tongue of the boot as this will slide your foot back and give you more room around your toes. (Many people forget to do this and so end up buying a boot that is too big for them.)

Thick socks are generally not needed with modern boots and I use just one ordinary pair, sometimes supplemented by a pair of very thin polypropylene inner socks for additional warmth (if you add too much thickness, you will impair circulation and end up making your feet colder). Because of this and because your feet swell in the warmth of the shop, I try on boots with very thin socks or bare feet – this will also allow for stretching. Work your feet inside the boots in the shop to see if there are any painful spots. Many shops will even allow you to take the boots away and if you decide to return them, they will only charge as though you hired them.

For those of you who suffer with your feet there are two solutions that you could consider, custom-fit boots and custom-fit footbeds. There are many systems of custom-fitting boots and most ski shops will stock one or other of them.

Footbeds are relatively new, but can make an incredible difference to your comfort and subsequently to your skiing. Again, a good ski shop will have a fitting service and if these do not work and you still have a real problem with your feet, consider going to a podiatrician and ask about orthotic footbeds. There are companies who will design a footbed specifically to your needs and although they are expensive I have found from personal experience that they are worth every penny you spend.

A further adjustment that can be made on some boots is canting. Jean-Claude Killy called this his 'secret weapon'. Most people are either slightly bow-legged or knock-kneed which means that it is very difficult to stand on flat feet in our boots. We either stand on the outside or the inside of our feet – and canting helps to correct this. It may also make monoskiing more comfortable, as your feet are locked in place, thus restricting any natural compensatory movements you might normally make.

These are the major features that you will find on ski-boots. The more you are prepared to pay, the more of them you find in the design. Remember that being comfortable and happy with your boots is essential to good skiing.

Clothing

The same criteria – being happy and comfortable – also apply to clothing. I believe, for example, that a new ski suit can actually help improve your skiing, through boosting your image of yourself; this increases your self confidence and so benefits your skiing. However, the reverse may be true for others and they may feel the need to dress down. I do not want to stress this point too far but it is important to feel mentally comfortable about what you are wearing.

It is of equal importance that your clothing does the job for which it is intended – keeping you warm and protected from the elements, whilst allowing complete freedom of movement. Because many of you are venturing into the powder for the first time, I will describe in some detail the type of clothing that is advisable. The environment can be very hostile and, as you well know, it is not all sunny days and clear blue skies. The temperature can easily drop to minus 20°C; add to this any wind and the wind-chill factor will reduce it still further. Your body must be protected from these extremes of temperature so that it can perform the highly skilful tasks asked of it, in safety. Let us start by looking at some of the materials presently on the market.

Of all the insulative materials available the best is still natural down. The problem is that it is very expensive and, should it get wet, it becomes a soggy mass with little insulative value. Many of the synthetic equivalents are close to down in performance, and since a new one appears every season I can only suggest that you compare the clo values. (A clo is a unit representing the insulative value of a material.)

For the outer skin we can choose between cottons, nylons and the revolutionary breathable waterproof fabrics. I have found the latter to be excellent at their best and at their worst not inferior to anything else. It is important not to expect too much from them, and to remember that they need careful handling. When they become dirty they will not work so well, and in some cold conditions any condensation will freeze, so blocking the pores through which the water vapour would normally pass. If you do sweat in them, it is probably because you are wearing too many clothes; if the body is too hot it will sweat in order to lose excess heat. Remember, they do not prevent you from sweating – they just allow the water vapour to escape, thus reducing the build-up of condensation. If you do choose a garment made of one of these breathable waterproof fabrics, be sure that all the seams are taped, or they will leak annoyingly.

Many manufacturers have started to use cotton fabrics again, but generally they are no cheaper and do not appear to have any great advantages over other materials – with one exception – if you fall on a steep hard slope, you are less likely to go hurtling down as the cotton fabrics have more friction than the nylon-based equivalents.

As well as protection from the elements, clothing must not restrict our movements and this is the first dilema that the designer must face.

All warm clothing relies on trapping still air as this offers the highest degree of insulation. If the clothing is too loose, you will move this still air as you move around, thus destroying some of its insulative value. Conversely, if it is too tight, it will restrict your circulation, which in turn will make your extremities cold. For this reason, my ideal clothing system is based on the principle that it must be well tailored. It should fit closely around the main body, usually with a belt or elastic waistband. The arms, shoulders and legs should allow a full range of movement without disturbing the main bodice and the air trapped inside it. This is particularly important in monoskiing, where many of the more advanced manoeuvres involve extremes of movement.

When you try on clothing, make sure you try on the whole system and put it through the complete range of movements you are likely to make when skiing. For example, if you are buying a separate jacket and pants, try them both on at the same time. There is nothing worse than finding that when you bend over the small of your back is bared. It is very important to keep this area protected as it is the place where your kidneys, which carry a lot of blood, are closest to the surface. A one-piece suit solves this problem, and I have been skiing in one for many years. I find that it is ideal for all but the very warmest of conditions. Providing that you can unzip the front, you can regulate the temperature quite well, and the value of a one-piecer in the powder speaks for itself. Having said that, however, remember that any snow that does get down your neck will have to travel the whole length of your body to escape, by which time it is cold water!

Basic Design Features

Whether you adopt a one- or two-piece system, there are some basic design features to look for. The collar should be large enough to allow your head to be covered up to the level of your mouth and perhaps as far as your nose. I have always found this feature far more satisfactory than a scarf, although many people do use scarves, particularly the silk ones to which the snow does not stick. I do not favour hoods that I cannot detach because when I fall over, especially in the powder, it fills up with snow and then it seems impossible to empty it without it going down your neck. The system I prefer is a thin windproof nylon hood which is stored within the collar of the garment. I then wear a normal ski hat and in the same compartment as the hood I store a motor cyclist's silk Balaclava for when the temperatures are really low. These can cover the whole face, leaving very little exposed skin (particularly if used with goggles). Inside the collar I like a second elasticated collar which sits snugly and comfortably around my neck and prevents those cold snowflakes from getting inside.

Any zips should have good covering flaps to prevent snow sticking to them and the wind blowing through. I like to have a number of pockets in which to store things, and I find the large cargo style pockets, out of harm's way on the legs, especially useful. These pockets must have adequate zips and covers otherwise they just collect snow. Velcro has a limited use as a fastening system on ski clothing because it very easily becomes clogged with snow and should therefore not be the only method employed.

Extra padding on the knees is much appreciated on long chair-lifts where the knees can become very stiff from the cold. Additional waterproofing on the seat is also welcome on those wet chairs.

There are a number of different systems to be found at the bottom of the trouser legs, which, as long as they are robust, keep out the snow, fit over the top of the boot and do not restrict leg movement when they are in place, should be fine.

Gloves

Cold hands can make you feel miserable even when everything else is marvellous. There are two main reasons for cold hands: the first is that the gloves are often too tight, hampering circulation, and the second is that they do not adequately protect the wrist where the blood supply is closest to the surface. Good glove systems used to be rare, but now there are several on the market that have an elasticated gauntlet which seems to serve the needs of the skier of deep snow very well. They also mean you do not need to fiddle around with velcro in order to get a good seal. Mitts are unquestionably warmer than gloves but I must admit I prefer the dexterity offered by gloves, unless it is very cold. Whichever you decide upon, ensure they are big enough and that they cover the wrist. You can supplement your gloves with thin liners but be sure (as with your boots) that the added thickness does not make them too tight. It is worth remembering that whenever you take your gloves off in cold conditions, you should first put them inside your jacket rather than on the ground or on the top of your ski pole and then, just before putting them back on, blow into them a couple of times – it is like putting on toasted gloves!

Underwear

Underneath these 'hi-tech' exterior garments our underwear has also changed. String vests and itchy woollen long johns are things of the past. The new breed of underwear will draw the sweat away from the skin, reducing that clammy feeling. These new polypropylene-based materials are certainly an improvement and most people find them very comfortable. However, wool is still one of the best insulators and if you really suffer from the cold, you can buy woollen vests and long johns which are much improved from the itchy things of the past.

Glasses and Goggles

Finally, a few words about your eyes and the need to protect them. I have seen many experienced skiers neglecting the protection of their eyes by not wearing glasses or goggles. Not only are the ultra-violet (and to a lesser extent the infra-red) rays damaging your eyes, but if you do get snow-blindness, which will result from not wearing glasses, a long way from the piste, you are in serious trouble and will be completely reliant upon your companions to get you down. This situation is serious when on two skis but on a mono – which is difficult to ski slowly – it is even worse.

Do not cut costs on goggles or glasses as many cheaper varieties do not provide adequate protection. When choosing goggles, I always go for the two lens variety, as I am convinced that they do not mist up as much. Moreover when you are monoskiing you need to be even more aware of the terrain than on two skis – you end up walking where you have misjudged the slope.

When you fall over in deep snow, your goggles and glasses always seem to become full of snow and so I carry a piece of lint soaked in a small amount of washing-up liquid with which I wipe my glasses clear. The detergent also helps to prevent further misting.

It is important that you do not skimp on any of these items because skiing off-piste involves many more hazards than ordinary, on-piste skiing. Good clothing can make an incredible difference, not just to your enjoyment but also to your very survival – and if I have not put you off, it is now time to go skiing.

2 The First Day

Now that you have equipped yourself, the time has come to head for the snow. The techniques that you try first will depend upon the conditions and your ability on two skis. I will describe the ideal situation first and deal with the alternatives later.

The Ideal Terrain

The most important consideration for your first attempt on the mono is to choose the correct terrain. Ideally, you want a slope covered in a layer of ankle-deep soft snow, on which you would be happy to schuss at speed. If it is too shallow, the ski will just wallow around and you will be continually catching edges. Beneath the soft layer the snow should not be too icy, otherwise the ski will break away on the turns. Make sure that the slope runs right to the bottom of the tow, as pushing yourself along with your poles is very hard work.

Although you may not be familiar with the off-piste, these slopes provide the best conditions (you must, however, read Appendix 1 on the dangers of avalanches beforehand). It is not as difficult as you may think to find such slopes and a smooth piste with a layer of soft snow can be just as good. If no such slopes are within easy reach, choose a smooth wide green or blue run, although if it is at all icy, you should wait until conditions improve, as in these conditions the mono is a very poor substitute for two skis, and you may become disillusioned with what is really a fun branch of the sport.

Lifts

You also need to consider the lifts, as drags are likely to cause problems until you have found your balance on the mono (*see* Chapter 3). The best type of lift is a cable or bubble car where it is not necessary to wear your ski. Innumerable systems for carrying the mono ski exist, so you will have to take your lead from the lift attendant.

If your chosen area is not served by a cable or bubble car, use a chair-lift. (A friendly partner and a sense of humour are also useful at this stage!) There are two ways in which you can tackle the chair: you can leave one foot out of the binding, which will help you to reach the take-off spot, or you can use your poles firmly to help you slide to it with both feet in place. Some lift operators do not like you using the former method, even though it is initially the easier of the two. Once aboard the chair, you will need to fix your foot into the binding if you have removed it.

Getting on the lift was, I am afraid, the easy part. Getting off is where the fun begins. The level of hilarity – at least for your friends and the other skiers around you – will depend upon the steepness and iciness of the exit ramp. Grasp both poles firmly as they will help you with your balance and, as the ramp approaches, get off the chair as if you had normal skis on, looking for a line that allows you to schuss to a stop; memories of those first few days of skiing will doubtless come flooding back! Never mind, it is all part of the fun, and you should soon get the hang of it.

Fig 4   Approaching a tow with one foot free.

The Basic Stance

Before you start to ski, remember the most important factors of a basic skiing stance. For your first few attempts at monoskiing, you should use the normal stance that you adopt on two skis, as this will work well for the turns I am about to describe and it will also be one less thing for you to think about. The more flamboyant mono-stance will be examined in the next chapter.

Feet

Let us look at this basic posture, starting with the feet. They are a major source of feedback about what is happening at one of the most important points, the contact zone between the ski and the snow. You may have been told to stand on your toes, your heels or even

the whole foot. Confusing, isn't it! In fact, all three positions can be valid, but to sort this confusion out, let us consider the concept of a neutral posture which is relaxed and balanced. In order to gain maximum feedback and better balance, you should adopt the middle position, where pressure is over the whole foot allowing you to move backwards or forwards. Most skiing will – with only one or two exceptions – call for pressure spread over the whole foot (although you may not always be aware of this). The idea of pressure, rather than weight, is used because people are better at relating to where they feel pressure than to where their weight is. The age-old shout of instructors to get your weight forwards usually means more forwards. In fact, they are trying to get your weight off your heels and the pressure over the whole foot.

Ankles

One frequently quoted saying of Continental ski-instructors is 'bend ze knees'; we do exactly that and as a result look as though we are sitting on the lavatory. What I believe they really want us to do is to bend our ankles; our knees will then bend naturally and our whole body will feel much more comfortable. You do not need to force your ankles forwards against the boots, just rest them lightly against the tongue. Flexing in this way also enables extension movements to take place and these are essential to many techniques.

Hips

Continuing up the body, I will miss out the knees because if your ankles are right your knees will look after themselves. The hips are quite an important region because they affect the upper body, and it is important that this remains as relaxed as possible so that it does not interfere with what the legs are trying to do. Stand upright and then hollow your back; can you feel the tensions in your back and shoulders? Now get rid of the hollow and see how this helps to relax the rest of the upper body. By getting rid of the hollowed back you will have tilted your pelvis upwards a little and this position allows a much more dynamic response to any athletic pursuits.

Head, Arms and Hands

The head is held up naturally so that you can see ahead. The factors which influence the position of your arms and hands are that they assist with your balance and pole planting. Climb up on to a chair, jump off and land as softly as possible; notice the position of your arms. Alternatively, try to balance on a narrow beam in a gym or on a kerb stone. In both these cases you will notice that your arms are being held out to the side and slightly in front of you (a little high perhaps

in the case of the jump). One of the best ways to describe this position is to imagine you are holding a hoop around your hips. If twelve o'clock is directly in front of you, then position your hands at ten o'clock and at two o'clock. This position should roughly correspond to the one you found yourself in earlier. Not only is it good for balance, but when you plant your poles you can do so with very little arm movement and in such a way that the forces transmitted by planting the pole will pass to the upper body via the bones and not stress any ligaments or tendons.

Most people have a particular part of their body which if they can relax it, helps to relax the rest of their body. When I am driving my car I often find myself gripping the steering wheel quite tightly, which in turn tenses my shoulders and neck and consequently makes me tired. If I relax my thumbs, it seems to act as a trigger and relaxes the rest of my shoulder girdle. When I am skiing the key lies in relaxing my shoulders; having discovered this, I now always give them a quick shrug as I set off down a run. Finding your key can only be done by trial and error and by listening to your body.

This then is our basic posture. Remember, it is not a rigidly held position but one from which we can move dynamically and return to if in need of balance.

Manoeuvres

Traversing

Probably the most difficult skill of all on a mono is simply standing still, especially if you are on a slight slope. The next most difficult skill has to be traversing; it is just like balancing on your uphill ski except that you cannot suddenly use the downhill ski. Try to balance over the middle of your foot, pull the outside (downhill) leg up towards you and use your poles to help maintain your balance. Alternatively, you can press down firmly on

Fig 5   Traversing. Pull up with the outside foot and slide it back in your boot.
Pressing down hard on the uphill foot may also help.

the heel of your uphill foot. If the ski turns uphill all the time, try shifting the pressure along your uphill foot (you may also find it useful to slide your downhill foot backwards within the boot).

This is probably a new sensation as it is not used in normal skiing, but because both your legs are fixed, you can slide your feet relative to each other inside your boots, even if they are very tight, and so create a turning force on the ski. You can even use this technique to turn on smooth shallow piste.

If you have to start turning before reaching your chosen slope, use the parallel turn you are most comfortable with; compression turns work well, as do small hop parallels. You may find a tendency for the ski to over-turn and for the tail to break away; this is usually caused

by your weight not being centrally over the ski or because your upper body is over-turning.

Side-Slipping

On occasions, you will need to side-skid on the mountain. This is achieved in much the same way as on two skis except that your balance is a little more critical as you will be skidding against the uphill edge. Control the edge with your knees as you would on two skis.

The Mono 'Kick Turn'

There are two ways in which you can kick turn on a mono. The first is simple in concept

Fig 6 Side-slipping. Use your poles to help with your balance.

Fig 7 Kick-turning on a mono. (*See* also Fig 8)

Fig 8   Lean back hard against the backs of your boots when kick-turning.

though quite hard in reality; you jump up and turn the ski through 180 degrees. The difficulty lies in the fact that it is quite hard to jump the whole ski off the ground because of its weight and because you have to launch yourself from the outside edge of the uphill foot. An easier method is to lean hard against the backs of your boots, lifting the tip of the ski in the process and swivelling around on the tail of the ski to face in the new direction. This is much easier than it looks, though you may lose a little distance down the slope, especially in steeper terrain.

The First Turns

Let us assume that somehow you have managed to reach your chosen slope. The techniques you use for your first attempts at turning will depend on how advanced a skier you are on two skis. If you can do compression turns (also known as avalement) try these first as they should not cause any real problems (see page 48). Once you feel comfortable with them, try other turns in any order, versatility being the name of the game. If you are not sure about compression turns, I suggest you try the following.

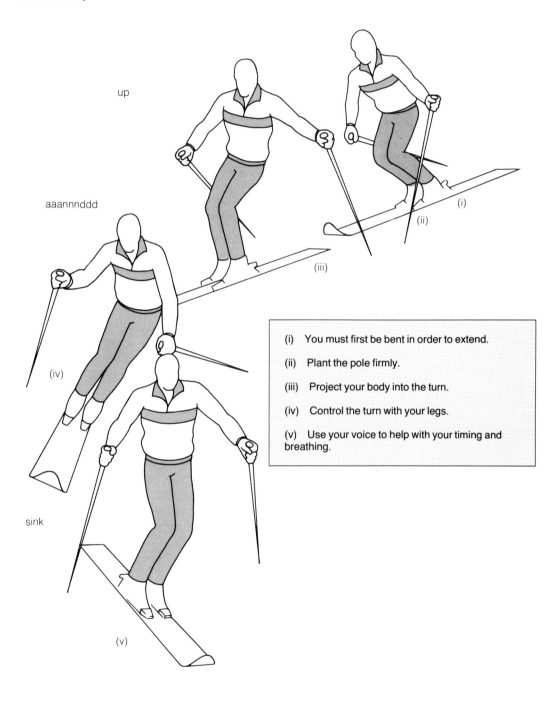

up

aaannnddd

sink

(i) You must first be bent in order to extend.

(ii) Plant the pole firmly.

(iii) Project your body into the turn.

(iv) Control the turn with your legs.

(v) Use your voice to help with your timing and breathing.

Fig 9 Leg extension turns.

The first thing that you will notice, especially if the snow is slightly heavy, is that the ski only feels stable once you are moving, much as a bicycle does. Similarly, a reasonable amount of speed is necessary before you attempt a turn (hence the importance in choosing a slope with which you are happy). A further conclusion to draw from this is that you must not let the ski lose too much speed in the turns; they must flow even more than on two skis.

Now for the turn itself (a leg extension turn). As I suggested earlier, for these early attempts you should adopt a stance as for normal skiing. Start in a very steep traverse and when you have picked up enough speed to feel stable, plant the pole and extend your legs, projecting your body into the turn at the same time. As the turn progresses sink down, controlling the arc of the turn with your knees. It sounds a lot to remember so let us look at each part separately:

1. *The pole plant.* This is exactly the same as in normal skiing, except that it is generally more effective on the mono, (at least to start with); a firm pole plant at the initiation of the turn will considerably aid the turn.

2. *The extension.* In order to extend, you first have to be bent, so be sure that in the traverse you adopt a normal skiing posture with your ankles flexed (this will ensure that your knees are also flexed) and a loose relaxed midrift. To extend, straighten your legs until you are standing on your toes inside your boots (many skiers are too lazy and do not extend fully). Having reached this point you then sink back, at the same speed as your extension, to your original position. (The movement is exactly as it would be on two skis and can, to a degree be practised in this manner.)

The rhythm of this bending and extending will be a major factor in determining the radii of your turns: a fast rhythm leading to a short radius and a slow rhythm to a large radius. You may find it useful to try to 'hang in mid-air' at the highest point of the extension as this will have the effect of allowing the ski to float towards the fall-line and prevent you from turning too quickly. The manoeuvre will be achieved more easily by staying up on your toes for a moment or two. This is an instance when using your voice can help you learn the proper technique.

Let us consider the words *up and sink* as descriptive of the movement we want to produce and that we want to try to 'hang in mid-air' in the middle of the manoeuvre. If we extend the word *and* to *aaannnddd*, drawing the word out, it has the effect of altering the timing of the actions. You can almost feel the actions, *up aaannnddd sink*. Try it – it may help you.

3. *Projecting yourself into the turn.* If you are finding it difficult to initiate the turn, it is likely that you are extending vertically upwards instead of up and into the turn. You should almost feel you are throwing yourself down the slope into the next turn. It therefore demands a high degree of commitment, but once mastered will help both your monoskiing and your normal skiing. As you extend, do so towards the centre of the next turn downhill from you and also rotate the upper body slightly in the direction of the new turn during the action.

4. *Control.* The last part of the turn is to control the radius of the turn with your knees. This is exactly the same as on two skis, except that you will be balanced over the uphill edge of the ski. If you find yourself over-turning, check that your uphill arm has not rotated behind you, taking your body with it. If it has, try to keep it in sight in front of you and rotate your body downhill a little more, almost to the point of anticipating the next turn. This anticipation will be used as a specific technique later, (*see* page 44). If you still find yourself overturning, start the next turn sooner so that one turn leads immediately into the next, setting up a continuous rhythm. Rhythm is absolutely vital in monoskiing and it will sort out many of the problems you may experience.

Fig 10   As the skier extends, notice how his body is projected into the new turn.

5. *Stance*. Finally, you may find that your legs become tired quite quickly. If so, check you are not sitting back too much. It is a common error and one which you must keep in mind. Whenever you feel yourself sitting back, shift your balance so that you can feel the pressure over the whole of your foot. The tendency to sit back too far will disappear once you begin to relax, and relaxation will come as you gain familiarity with the mono. In all sports you are told to relax more, but it is, of course, very difficult – I believe it can only be achieved when you have done enough of the activity (though

you should try the ideas mentioned at the beginning of the chapter, as they may well help). If your legs are feeling wobbly, try holding your knees tightly together. Later, when your balance has improved, you will be able to relax them again.

If these ideal conditions do not exist, you will find yourself trying the mono for the first time on a prepared piste. The above turns will work, but you should concentrate on using your knees to control the mono. The turns should be shorter but still in a continuous rhythm and with a strong pole plant; some anticipation of the turn will help its

Fig 11   Practising on a smooth, soft piste.

initiation. The control will come from a powerful swing to the hill which, even though you will be on the outside edge of the uphill leg, will be similar to a swing to the hill on two skis. Depending upon the type of mono you are using, you may find it helpful to allow the pressure under your feet to shift during the turn from the front to the back. This is quite different from sitting back, when you will feel the back of the boot actually digging into your leg. I will expand upon this idea in the next chapter.

All these turns are very useful and will work in most snow conditions. Once you are comfortable with one or other, it is time to experiment further and to explore the possibilities of the mono.

Falling

The mono is as safe to ski as normal skis. The only type of injury that might occur more frequently will happen at slow speeds, when your knees could dig into the snow as you fall. Any risk of this will be eliminated if you straighten your legs as you fall – and anyway it will not occur if the forces are

Fig 12   Getting up.

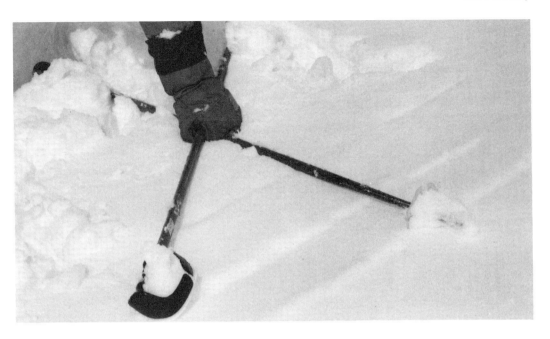

Fig 13   Notice the use of the crossed poles.

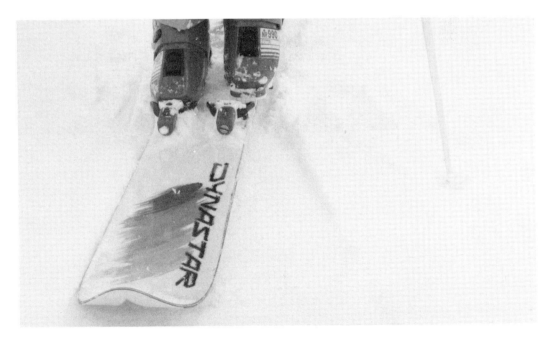

Fig 14   Putting your ski back on. Refit the top boot first and then the downhill boot.

sufficient to release the binding. You are also less likely to damage the inside ligaments of your knees as you will rarely catch the inside of your leg (as may happen on two skis). This is not to say that injuries will not occur but that they will be no more frequent than in normal skiing.

Having fallen, you may find it difficult to get back up again, especially in deep snow. First, try to regain your feet just as you would with two skis by placing your ski at 90 degrees to the fall-line. You can help yourself by crossing your poles to give yourself more support as you push up. If the bindings have released then clear the loose snow and re-engage the uphill foot first. This is the opposite of the method for two skis.

From time to time, in deep snow, I have fallen over and found it really difficult to get back up by any normal method and on these occasions I have shifted my body over the ski, swung it into the fall-line and allowed it to start sliding down the hill. As it picked up speed, I pulled myself into the upright position – a fairly strenuous procedure, but when all else fails, it is worth a try.

3 Day Two

I hope that your first day was reasonably successful. Falls, no doubt, were frequent, but do not despair. The subtleties of balance on the mono soon come with a little perserverance. If you have had some success with the techniques described in the previous chapter, it is time to try some new ones.

The Drag-Lift

If you have begun to find your balance on the mono, you can now have a go at riding a drag-lift. It is not as drastic as you might think, but make sure you choose a fairly shallow and slow lift for your first attempts. Particularly avoid those which tend to send you airborne at the start. I vividly remember my first attempt; I grabbed the poma, put it between my legs and off I shot. After about two metres I felt my balance going, but I was determined not to lose face in front of the crowd of pisteurs that had gathered for some fun at my expense. So I jumped up in an effort to gain some semblance of control, did two 360s and, to my amazement, landed straight on the track again. There were cheers of approval from my onlookers, but my jubilation was short-lived – around the next corner I fell off completely. I skied down amidst much laughter to try again.

One solution which used to gain more acceptance than it does today is to use a small ski, a little longer than a boot and put it on one foot with the other on the mono, so making riding the drag-lifts easy (and at the end you simply clamp the ski between your feet). This method, however, has lost favour, probably because it only takes a little practice before you can ride the drag-lifts without the encumbrance of another ski.

The method that I generally use works as follows. Approach the drag lift with the hand closest to it free, the other hand holding one pole firmly by its grip and the spare pole at half height. Grab the poma as normal and immediately put it between your legs – the next few moments are the most difficult, as the poma speeds up and you start to ascend. Hold the bar firmly and use your pole forcibly to retain your balance. As the poma advances, turn the mono obliquely across

Fig 15   The drag-lift. The ski is diagonally across the track, one hand is on the bar and the other holds both poles and helps by planting one of them to maintain balance.

37

your path so that it is skidding slightly (the direction will depend upon the camber of the slope, the tip of the ski pointing up the camber). You should now feel more comfortable and with a little concentration should have no trouble reaching the exit which is tackled as per normal, though it is useful to have a pole in each hand as you slide clear. This method is particularly good when the track is rutted.

When you are comfortable with this method you can try riding the drag-lifts with a pole in each hand rather than holding on to the bar, which is slightly less tiring. With the mastery of the drag-lift the whole ski area will now be open to you.

The Mono-Stance

Before examining some of the other turns let us first look at the two stances in more detail. Up to now I have recommended that you use

Fig 16   The drag-lift. Use both poles for balance and ride it with the ski straight.

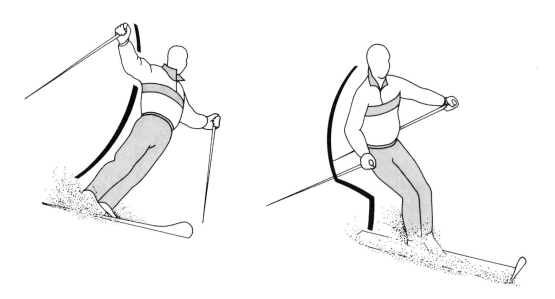

Fig 17   Left: the mono stance, right: the normal stance.

Fig 18   Normal skiing stance.

Fig 19 Monoskiing stance.

your normal ski stance, and having had some success, you can now look at what is called the mono-stance. This stance is much higher, being suitable for the long cruising turns in deep and difficult snow where the mono excels. Your ankles remain flexed forward, but the knees straighten slightly and the hips are projected forwards, though the pelvis remains tilted upwards as in normal skiing. The arms are held high and spread out for balance. This position will feel strange at first, seemingly contradicting many of the points I have made about the basic stance, but it does work well on the

mono in many situations. Indeed many expert monoskiers use nothing else. Personally, I recommend that you try both, building up your skill level so that you can use each as the situation demands. I believe that versatility is the hallmark of the accomplished skier, whichever particular 'ski game' he or she is playing.

Angulation

At this stage it is worth looking at the ways in which the ski can be put on to its edge, as

Fig 20   Knee angulation.

Fig 21   Hip angulation.

Fig 22 Banking.

this will be of great importance in examining the different turns to be tried. The ski can be put on edge by 'angulating' the body in three ways, using the knees, the hips or the whole body (known as banking). It would be wrong to suggest that any one method was any better than another – they are just different, each lending itself to particular methods of turning. (In Fig 23 you can see that the three methods also tend to dictate the radius and frequency of the turns.)

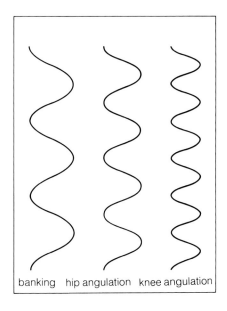

banking hip angulation knee angulation

Fig 23 Different angulation can lead to differing radii and frequencies of turns.

Fig 24   Notice the different radius of the turn with hip angulation.

Fig 25   Notice the different radius of the turn with banking.

Fig 26   Turning without using anticipation.

Fig 27   Turning with anticipation; notice the body pre-turning towards the new direction.

Anticipation

Anticipation is occasionally used and is a technique which can help in several ways. I have already mentioned that if you find the ski over-turning, you can prevent this by pre-turning your upper body towards the next turn – anticipating it. Anticipation also helps when it is difficult to turn the ski, in heavy snow for example, or when you need to turn quickly, such as in the moguls. It can be applied to most turns regardless of whether you are using a normal stance or a mono-stance.

The Jump Turn

As with two skis the jump turn is very versatile and particularly useful for the monoskier if you do not want to pick up too much speed. However, because you must take off on the uphill foot it has its limitations.

For the jump, two leg actions can be used; the extension and the retraction. You can also jump the front of the ski up, the whole of the ski or the back of the ski. On the mono you normally use the leg extension action to lift the back of the ski (the other combinations are possible but tend to require greater effort).

Before examining the use of the jump turn in monoskiing, the concept of the flow-line needs to be explained. Whatever turns you do, you will probably feel moments when you are flowing and moments when you are resisting. The line on which the turn begins to flow is known as the flow-line and it often, but not necessarily, coincides with the fall-line. The fall-line is often likened to the line down which a ball would roll, but, if that ball meets a slope it will continue up that slope under its momentum before returning to the fall-line. The ball actually follows its flow-line and not the fall line. Being able to feel the point in a turn at which the ski begins to flow will help make your skiing smoother, a vital component of monoskiing.

For your first attempts at the jump turn, go back to the slope you used on the first day. Head down the slope and gently swing to the hill. As the pressure builds up under your feet plant your downhill pole and, extending your legs, quickly hop the tail of the ski into the flow-line. (At this speed it will coincide with the fall-line but as you go faster you will feel its position change.) Land as softly as you can and swing to the hill in the new direction, preparing for the next turn. As with leg extension turns, mentioned in the previous chapter, your hop should be up and into the new turn with a slight twisting of the upper body. If you experience difficulty

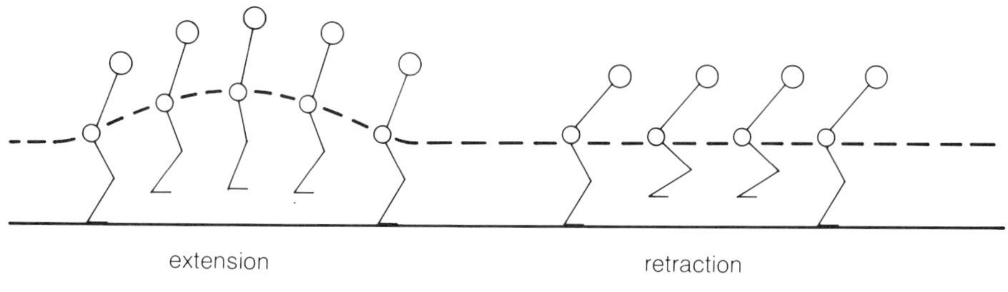

extension   retraction

Fig 28   Extension and retraction jumps.

Fig 29   A jump turn.

with these turns, concentrate on the finish of the previous turn rather than the jump phase of the new turn, as the problem probably lies in having no positive platform from which to jump, rather than in the actual jump itself. Again, the use of words may prove useful. If you say the word 'jump' as a cue, it needs to be said firmly; saying it softly will result in a soft action.

Short Swings

The short swing is an extension of the jump turn and now the mono is being taken onto steeper and steeper terrain, so this technique has become more important. Those who are familiar with the technique should be aware of the different types of short swinging; all are possible on the mono but I prefer those which use leg extensions and rotate about a point half-way between the tip of the ski and your boot. If you do not know how to short swing, I would suggest that the mono is not the ski to learn on; it would be better to learn on two skis.

Jump turns in all their guises have their place in your repertoire but do not spend too much time on them as they do not really exploit the full potential of the mono.

(i)   Check firmly.

(ii)   Rebound from the check and jump the tail back into the fall-line.

(iii)   Swing the ski around again, anticipate the next turn and check.

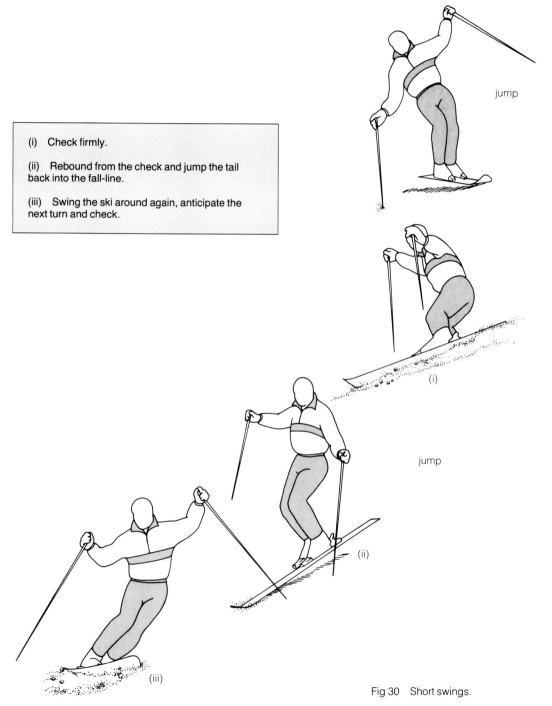

jump

(i)

jump

(ii)

(iii)

Fig 30   Short swings.

47

Compression Turns

The compression turn, as well as being one of the most useful techniques on two skis, is also a very good way of turning with the mono. If you are already familiar with this technique you should have no problems in adapting it to the mono, but if you have not come across it before then do not worry, because it is as easy to learn on a mono as it is on two skis.

The best way to learn is to find some small bumps and to practise absorbing them. Using the normal skiing stance, choose a slow traverse angle and imagine you are carrying a tray of very valuable cut-crystal glasses – or trying to balance a book on your head. The object of the exercise is to ski across the bumps, keeping your upper body at a constant level. You do this by allowing your legs to bend and stretch through the crest and hollows. Initially, this is a passive action; as your ski hits the bump you allow your knees to rise up towards your chest until the top is reached and then you extend your legs into the next trough, keeping the ski in contact with the snow throughout. As you go faster, so the action becomes more and more active with you positively pulling your legs up and pushing them down until you reach such a speed that you are virtually pre-jumping each bump – this is almost taking you into the realms of the specialist bump skier, requiring considerable fitness and perfect timing. If you find it difficult to traverse without side skidding do not worry – the exercise will still work.

Now let us try a turn; find a small bump and approach it as before, only this time when you reach the crest, rotate the ski into the new direction and extend your legs as before. Feel the tension in your stomach and thigh muscles when your body is folded and notice the feeling of turning power that comes from having your legs in this position. This action will be helped by planting the pole slightly on the downhill side of the bump. Planting the pole late in this way will help delay the moment you begin to turn your legs. People often turn too early when they first try these turns but this does not make full use of the shape of the bump. One

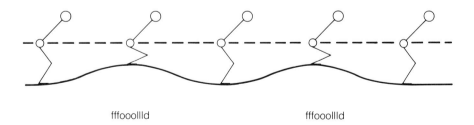

fffooollld   fffooollld

Fig 31 Absorbing bumps. The head and hips stay level and the legs flex in order to absorb the terrain. Use your voice to help with breathing and timing, extending the words to extend the action.

Fig 32   Mogul skiing. Notice the amount of absorption and the pole plant.

of the advantages of these turns is that they can be done fairly slowly and, because of the extra rotational leverage your thighs have when the knees are bent at 90 degrees, it is a very powerful way of turning.

These turns require practice because the leg movement may be quite different from what you are accustomed to doing; it will be more difficult to maintain an edge on the mono, which means you may have to take a steeper line than you would on two skis. You may find that it takes a while to stop standing up on top of the bump. If so, try doing the turn very slowly, making sure your head stays level with your pole-planting hand at the crest of the mogul. Alternatively, visualise someone in front of you and freeze-frame him at the crest; feel the tension in your thighs, notice the position of your hands and sense the tightness of your stomach muscles.

You may feel only one of these sensations, but visualise it several times and then perform the manoeuvre. Another method might be to use your voice, so as you approach the mogul say to yourself, perhaps out loud for the first few times *ffooollldddd*, stretching the word out as you go over the bump. As you go faster sharpen up the word and say it louder as the action becomes more explosive; *FFOLLD!* This will not only remind you of the required action, but will help both with the timing and with your breathing. With practice, you will find that the moguls can be skied quite well on a mono though I doubt you will ever feel as comfortable as you would on two skis because of the lack of independent leg action.

Once you have become reasonably comfortable turning in the bumps, try the same

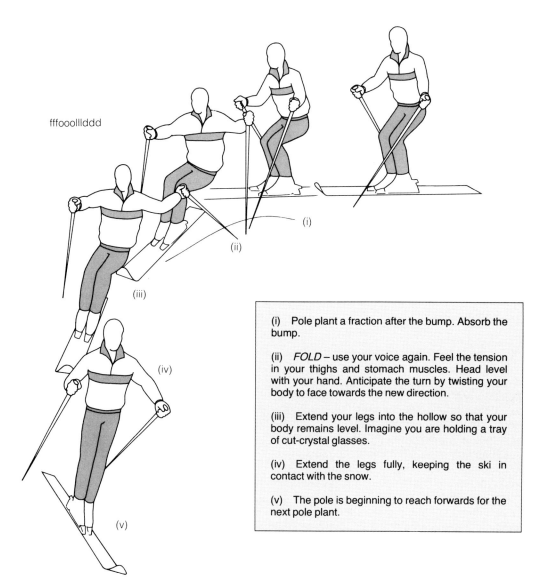

fffooolllddd

(i) Pole plant a fraction after the bump. Absorb the bump.

(ii) *FOLD* – use your voice again. Feel the tension in your thighs and stomach muscles. Head level with your hand. Anticipate the turn by twisting your body to face towards the new direction.

(iii) Extend your legs into the hollow so that your body remains level. Imagine you are holding a tray of cut-crystal glasses.

(iv) Extend the legs fully, keeping the ski in contact with the snow.

(v) The pole is beginning to reach forwards for the next pole plant.

Fig 33   Compression turns.

Fig 34   Skiing the moguls at speed.

in deep snow. Start in the fall-line in a low position and extend your legs as you swing to the hill. At the end of the swing retract your legs, turn the ski and extend your legs against the new edge. Rhythm is vital and controlling your breathing may help. You can use words again to assist, or you can breathe out forcibly at each extension of the legs (it is much easier to control your breathing on exhalation than on inhalation). With practice you will find the compression turn to be one of the most useful and versatile of techniques, whatever type of ski you are on.

Hip Rolling Turns

There are three subtle variations of this same compression idea. I will call them simply knee rolling, hip rolling and banking turns. All of them are initiated in a similar way but in each you concentrate upon a different part of the body and by so doing you alter the turns slightly; let us start with the hip rolling turns.

Choose a large wide run, preferably with a layer of soft snow on it, and start to schuss down the flow-line (which is, for the moment, the fall-line). When you are going quite fast, drop your right hip to the right and as you turn, move your hips back over gradually to the left, keeping them level as you do so. For a moment or two the ski will continue along its previous path (the flow-line) because of its momentum and will then, as the edge of the ski bites into the snow, begin to flow into the next turn. Repeat this with a steady tempo, and after several turns you should have established a relaxing

Day Two

(a)

(b)

(c)

Fig 35   Hip rolling turns.

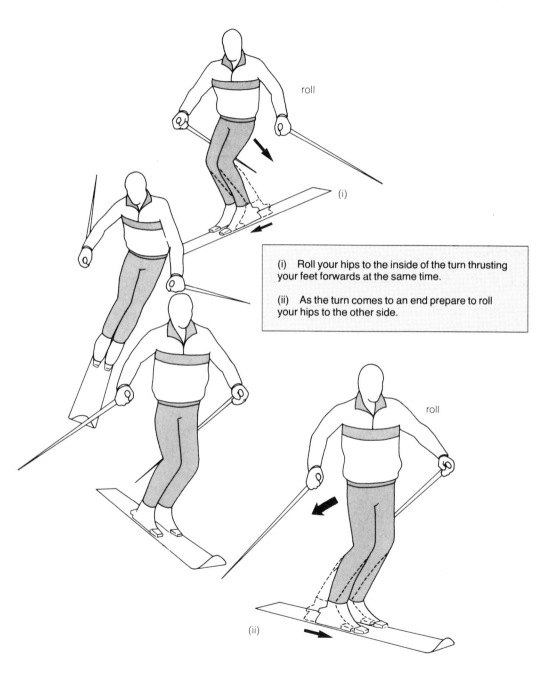

(i)   Roll your hips to the inside of the turn thrusting your feet forwards at the same time.

(ii)   As the turn comes to an end prepare to roll your hips to the other side.

Fig 36   Hip rolling turns with foot thrusting.

rhythm. You should feel as though you are rolling your hips from one side to the other to initiate the turns. This, of course, assumes that the rest of your basic technique is good. If it does not feel easy, try dropping your hips even further into the turns, moving sooner from one to the next, so making use of the flow-line or the momentum from the previous turn. This feeling – of the last turn flowing into the next – is a sensation that, once felt, will not be forgotten since it feels so positive and satisfying. These turns are really not hard if you can muster the necessary commitment, although in some types of snow you will need to be very sensitive to the pressure under your feet as the ski flows beneath you. If you are keeping your hips level you will find that this pressure remains almost constant throughout the turn, unless you turn very sharply when the ski may become airborne.

These turns provide an excellent opportunity to experiment with a technique known as foot thrusting which not only enhances the feeling of control but also allows you to use the edge of the ski more positively. As you start the new turn, thrust your feet forwards through the turn so you feel that you are accelerating your ski around the curve. The pressure will start on the heels (from the previous turn), move to the middle and then to the balls of the feet. To complete the turn, move your feet forwards to feel the pressure in the middle and so on. This is actually a very useful technique; once you have felt it in these turns, try to introduce it to the other turns.

After you have practised them with a normal stance, try them with the mono stance – which should work just as well (especially if you employ the foot thrusting technique). Rhythm is again essential and the resulting flowing turns will be a real pleasure.

Knee Rolling Turns

The second variation on these compression turns are knee rolling turns. Return to the same slope. Start down the fall line and roll your knees from side to side with a steady rhythm. The first few turns, as always, will feel cumbersome, but as you let the rhythm take over, so the turns begin to take care of themselves, your legs feel as if they are made of rubber and the ski almost turns by itself. It is essential to move quickly from one turn to the next as any hesitation – no matter how uncomfortable or unusual it might feel – will lose the turn. The result is a fast, flowing, edgy turn which makes you feel that you are using the ski to its maximum advantage. You should feel the ski snaking below you, almost (but not quite) out of control. It demands a loose and supple body and a word of warning is necessary; these turns can stress your knees to a considerable degree, so do not attempt them unless you are very fit and regularly ski fast and hard. These are only really possible in a normal skiing stance as the mono stance does not allow you to move your knees sufficiently.

Banking

Banking, however, lends itself ideally to the mono stance and you may indeed prefer it to the normal stance. These turns, given good conditions (deep snow) are simplicity itself. Extend your legs, bank the whole body over and the turn will happen. The trick is to know when to pull out of the turn and start the next one; leave it too late and the result will be spectacular.

The advantage of using the mono stance is two-fold; firstly you will feel as though you can steer the turn using the centre of your body, as though the power for the turn comes from your hips. This idea is difficult to communicate, but it is a sensation similar to the one you will have felt when foot thrusting, except that in this case you project the ski

(a)

(b)

(c)

Fig 37   Knee rolling turns.

Fig 38   Banking.

around the curve using your hips instead of your feet. Once you have felt it you will know because you will feel the power and control of the turn coming from this area of your body. Secondly, it allows you to ski with the pressure on your heels without it turning you excessively. In many types of snow this will make the mono easier to turn as it lifts the front of the ski clear of the snow. This, however, is not the same as leaning against the backs of your boots – which will always feel tiring.

If you experience difficulty with this turn, it will be either because you are not going fast enough for the amount of banking that you are trying, or because you are holding on to the turn for too long. This turn requires a lot of speed, so begin on a slope where you can let it build up gradually. Solving the second problem can only be done by trial

and error. If you keep crashing at the end of the turn, try throwing yourself into the next turn much sooner. You will also find that this turn works extremely well in bad snow such as crust, and in Chapter 4 I will expand upon this further.

Surf Turns

A further development of the compression turn is the surf turn. It was so called by the French ski teacher Georges Joubert because he and his students thought it resembled the stance adopted by surfers and skateboarders. Sometimes, when you use compression turns at speed in deep, difficult snow, you may find that the ski becomes uncontrollable and starts to leap out of the snow, sending you airborne on

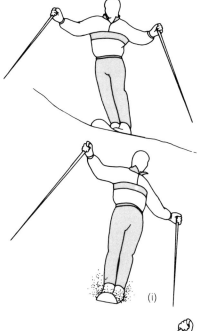

(i) Extend with a strong rotation and projection into the turn.

(ii) Power through the turn with your hips.

Fig 39   Mono turns with leg extension and banking.

Fig 40   Normal stance. Compare this with Fig 41.

Fig 41   Surf stance. Notice how flat the ski is and how the knees are rolled outwards.

every turn. If this happens, the solution may be to use the surf turn. The difference lies mainly in the stance; a surf stance allows you to control the edge more subtly which prevents the ski from overturning at speed – one of the problems that occurs when it leaps out of the snow. You should experiment, either in deep, difficult snow or in the moguls with the control that this stance allows you. If you use the moguls, ski down the valleys, braking as little as possible and you will almost automatically adopt a surf stance just to remain in control. Because of its subtleties, this turn is difficult to describe and you must learn it by experimenting with your stance until you almost feel your ankles (not the knees) controlling the turn.

Using the turns described in this chapter you should be able to appreciate the mono for the fun machine that it is, whether you have taken it off-piste or not. Most devotees, however, would probably agree that the mono really comes into its own when it is taken away from the crowds and into the trackless areas of the off-piste. Its use in these conditions will be considered in the next chapter, but first a few situations that may cause problems should be covered.

Ice

Tackling icy patches will always be awkward, whatever ski you have. If you are new to monoskiing and not yet hooked, it is probably best to leave it behind when such conditions prevail or you may become discouraged. If you do come across an icy area, you can tackle it in two ways: firstly, you can simply schuss it, hoping that you can regain control on the other side or else you can side-slip it, working hard with your poles to maintain your balance.

Bad Visibility

Another situation when the mono should be left behind is in conditions of poor visibility. It is not because the mono is any harder to use than normal skis in these conditions, but because you cannot see the lie of the land, and will probably find yourself involved in a lot of walking – which can be very frustrating. If you are sure of your routes, skiing in these conditions can be a good exercise, as it will help to develop your senses (other than sight), which in turn will make your skiing more sensitive and your skills more complete. Try using rhythmical compression turns, dragging your poles so that you get feedback from them as to how fast you are going. These turns give you maximum feedback about what is happening under your feet and also allow you to absorb any terrain you have been unable to anticipate.

Trees

Trees often harbour the best powder, where it will not have been destroyed by the wind, and so they offer a great temptation to the monoskier. In these conditions the mono can be great fun, but remember that it cannot generally be turned as quickly as two skis, especially when a tree root looms up suddenly and as you will probably be skiing a little faster on a mono than on two skis, this will accentuate the problem! As on two skis, it is also wise to remove your hands from the pole straps in case the pole gets caught on a branch.

Going Back to Two Skis

The transition back to two skis should not cause any problems providing you have been skiing the mono properly. However, some people tend to crank the mono around in the turns because they do not prepare correctly for the turn; this can be a problem

lift aanndd sink

(i)

(ii)

(iii)

(i)   You must be going fast. Retract the downhill leg. Do not straighten the uphill leg but rather bend it down further while lifting the other one. *LIFT* and *SINK*.

(ii)   *Think* about getting to the new position, the point to which you want the turn to take you.

(iii)   Shuffle forwards the foot you have lifted.

Fig 42   Foot lifting turns – the best turn to use when returning to two skis.

if transferred to two skis. The main difference between the two disciplines is that in monoskiing your feet are clamped and as a result your body is not in quite the usual position. When I return to two skis, I overcome this by first trying footlifting turns with a strong shuffle action; this accentuates the independent leg action which is so important on two skis, and which clearly highlights the differences between the mono and two skis technique.

4 Advanced Techniques

Now that you handle the mono a little better it is time to show you the real potential of the ski. Not only will you have to polish your techniques but you will also have to abandon some preconceived ideas about the terrain. In the words of its designer, Mike Doyle:

'. . . you look at the terrain totally differently to the skier. You start looking at the side walls and the lips and how to get your feet higher than your head . . . '

This, for many, is one of the great attractions of the mono; this different view of the way you ski can be incorporated into our normal skiing, which in turn can open up new areas of terrain and experience. The other great attraction is that the mono is great off-piste in bad snow conditions, where even the best and most committed off-piste skier finds it hard to enjoy normal skiing. All of this may sound intimidating and even a little esoteric, but bear with me because it is really not as hard as it may at first appear; there is no reason why these techniques should be the preserve of only the wild and crazy skiers of the movies. Even more important, they are great fun!

Straight-Lining

The first technique to show you can also be performed on two skis, though it is better on the mono. It is known as straight-lining. Many of you will have seen in the movies skiers with bizarre names such as 'Ted Shred' tearing straight down slopes at breakneck speed, leaning right back, with the front of the ski becoming airborne. Well,

this is what you are going to try, only you will be let into it gently.

You will need to find a slope on which you would normally be happy to schuss fast and which has an easy run-out. The condition of the snow is not critical, although soft snow to the height of your boots would be ideal (you should not try it on piste or on very firm snow). Start going down in a normal schuss and as the speed picks up, begin to lean against the backs of your boots. As the speed increases further, so the air will start to catch under the front of the board and lift it clear of the snow. You can actually control your speed to a degree by leaning back even harder and digging the tail of the board into the snow. Eventually you will find that only the very back of the ski is in contact with the snow but your speed will have levelled out and, provided you do not make any sudden movements, you will feel balanced. As with many advanced skiing techniques you will not be able to stop instantly and so may feel out of control. Being able to cope with this feeling will advance your skiing ability a long way and what you have to do is to realise that you *will* be able to stop at the end of the run (providing that you have chosen a sensible place to ski) and to relax in that thought, even though you cannot stop before the end.

There are actually many occasions in skiing when this mentality is essential in order to ski confidently and smoothly. Once you have tried this a few times and are finding your confidence, lean back even further, arching your back so that your head reaches the snow behind (definitely a soft snow game!) – the French call this 'sham-pooing'. Apart from being fun this technique does have its uses and can often be the

Fig 43   Straight-lining. Notice how the ski is only touching at its tail.

Fig 44   Straight-lining. Once mastered, this technique offers great excitement.

easiest way to descend when the conditions are particularly bad. Let us head further into these bad conditions, not because I want to give you a hard time, but because it is in breakable crust and heavy snow that the mono really excels and it is there that you are most likely to appreciate its virtues.

Skiing Difficult Snows

Breakable Crust

The nightmare of snow types has to be breakable crust. It comes in several different guises, depending upon how it was formed. Sometimes it will break consistently and at other times it will break when you least expect it. It can be formed by the wind or by the action of the sun and a subsequent freeze. Whichever way it is formed, it seems to give normal skis a mind of their own, each ski continually wanting to go in a different direction. It can, of course, be skied well on two skis, but on mono it can also be enjoyed!

The first skiing concept to be abandoned is the desire to go down, turning regularly. There is another way – which I have already hinted at – which is to ski the terrain like a big-dipper ride, where you accelerate into the bowls only to slow down again as you rise up to the top of the next mound. Your tracks will be long and smooth, following the lie of the land. It is a very graceful way of skiing and can be tremendously satisfying. If the crust is thin and breaking consistently, try leg extension mono turns, but be sure to keep your speed up. Imagine you are at the top of a run, before you a wide open slope of moderate steepness, the visibility good and the slope covered in a number of small gullies and hillocks which form banks of snow on which you will be able to turn. As you descend into the first bowl, pick up speed and, feeling the crust breaking below the ski, adjust your position so that its tip is clear of the snow but so that you are still relaxed. In front of you is a bank with the slope heading off to your left; as you begin to climb it and your speed drops, prepare to turn. Let the terrain dictate the radius of the turn (which must in any case be large) and as you head back towards the valley look for the next bank and plan another long cruise around it, using the land to control your descent. Providing you keep your movements smooth and fluid, you should be able to ski this type of crust with comparative ease. If you experience difficulties, you are probably either going too slowly or trying to turn too quickly.

If the crust is breaking inconsistently, you may find it more comfortable to do long compression turns, adopting a lower stance and using the hip rolling technique. This should make you feel more stable and allow you to adapt to the changes in the snow more easily. By being very sensitive to the pressure under your feet you may be able to keep the ski on the surface most of the time. Sudden movements will tend to make the ski break through and with experience you may even be able to read the snow, spotting slight textural differences that indicate whether or not the snow will collapse under your weight.

Sometimes the snow is so crusty and the angle of the slope so gentle that turns, even on a mono, are very difficult. This difficulty arises because you cannot pick up enough speed. When you meet these conditions you must simply accept them and schuss downhill, avoiding any temptation to turn – which is surprisingly difficult! Straight-lining can be useful in these situations.

Wet Snow

The other notorious condition is wet, heavy snow that seems, to quote Mike Doyle again, 'to suck at the sole of your ski making it very difficult to turn'. A variety of techniques will work, but especially efficient are hip rolling turns and, once again, mono-stance leg extension turns. Sometimes, depending upon your speed or the steepness of the

Fig 45   Mono turns in the crust. Notice the projection of the body into the turn.

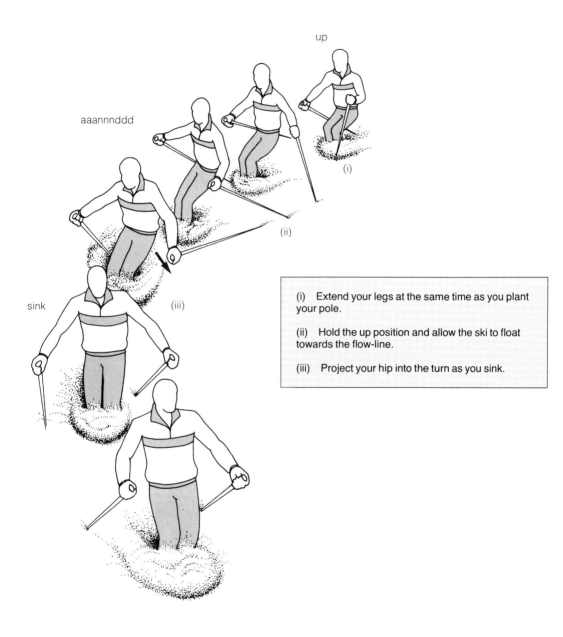

up

aaannnddd

sink

(i)

(ii)

(iii)

(i) Extend your legs at the same time as you plant your pole.

(ii) Hold the up position and allow the ski to float towards the flow-line.

(iii) Project your hip into the turn as you sink.

Fig 46   Leg extension turns in the powder.

slope, the ski will grab and turn very sharply, causing you to compress very aggressively to prevent your becoming airborne with each turn. If you find this throws you out of control, try some surf turns as they may give you a little more control over your edges and, by softening them, you can avoid the sudden reactions between ski and snow that are the cause of the problem.

Powder

The ideal snow is, of course, powder snow and here again the mono ski excels. Hopefully, you will already have had some experience of the shallower powder snows during your introduction to monoskiing. If not, find a slope of moderate steepness and with a depth of snow of anything between your ankles and your knees. Start with some large radius turns, using leg extension turns and plenty of rhythm; at this stage·one turn must link into the next in order to prevent the ski from over-turning. As you shorten the radius you may be able to eliminate some of the extension in favour of hip rolling turns. The athletic amongst you can take this further and experiment with knee rolling turns – but be careful as they put a lot of stress on your knees.

As the slope gets steeper I would suggest (unless, of course, you like going very fast) that you try some compression turns. Head down the fall-line and swing to the hill and as you complete the swing, pull your knees up towards your chest, turning the skis at the same time. When the speed starts to

Fig 47   Compression turns in the powder.

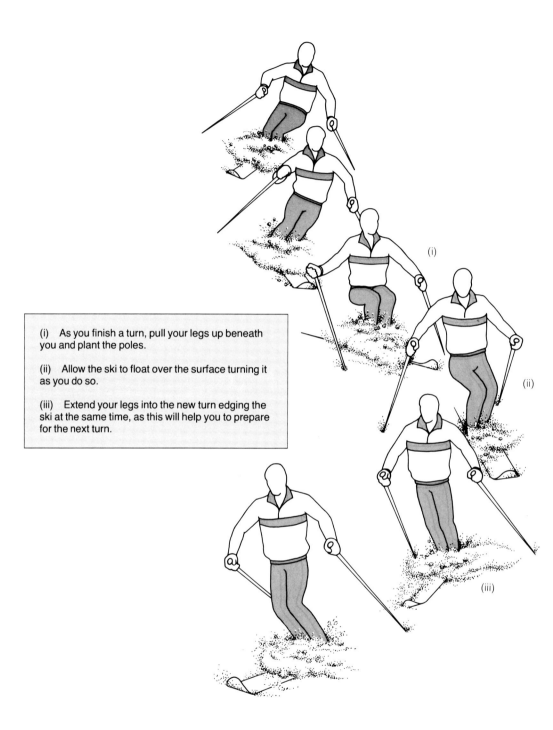

(i) As you finish a turn, pull your legs up beneath you and plant the poles.

(ii) Allow the ski to float over the surface turning it as you do so.

(iii) Extend your legs into the new turn edging the ski at the same time, as this will help you to prepare for the next turn.

Fig 48 Compression turns in the powder.

increase, extend your legs into the new turn, making sure the ski is edged. It is important to edge the ski because it will then react to the snow, causing it to rise to the surface, so making less work for you. As your speed increases still further you may find the ski over-reacting as it did in heavy snow; it will then be time to try the surf turn again.

All of these turns will result in classic, linked turns of varying radii which work in all depths of snow, though a deeper covering may require more practice. For these conditions, you will have to ski more subtly and be sensitive to the pressure under your feet; timings may also have to be slowed down a little in order to let the ski react to the snow. Again, in deeper snow, you must maintain enough speed for the ski to float to the surface; otherwise the front will dig in and, to compensate, you will start to lean back which will tire you very quickly.

Once you are happy with these conditions it is time to move on again. First you should try some high speed cruising (just as you did in the crust), looking for banks and hollows with which to control your speed – and then there are a number of new and exciting manoeuvres that you can try.

Advanced Manoeuvres

Upsidedowners

As the name implies the object of the manoeuvre is to turn off a bank at speed so that the ski ends up above your head and you continue to turn. The important factor here is the speed – you need plenty of it. Normally you would choose a line up the bank so that your speed died as you climbed, but on this occasion, however, choose a lower line so that you loose very little speed. As you cruise high across the bank throw your body and hips down the slope; the ski will remain high above you and, providing you have sufficient speed, you will do a classic hip rolling turn – except

Fig 49 Upsidedowners. The skier tries to turn so that his feet end up above his head. A lot of speed and commitment is needed.

it will be in a different plane. If you find that you have lost speed you may still be able to salvage the turn by finishing as though performing a compression turn.

Tail-Stalling

This is really quite easy once you get the timing right. Cruise up a bank until your speed drops right down and as you stall throw your weight back onto the tail of the ski, twisting the tip back downhill at the same time. When you are accomplished at these, try a 360 tail-stall. For this, rather than rotate the front of the ski the natural way (back down the slope), rotate it uphill and then all the way round, so that you complete a 360 turn.

Fig 50   Tail-stalling. The skier shoots up the bank to the point of stall, leans hard against the backs of his boots and lifts the tip of the ski into the air . . .

Fig 51   . . . then he twists quickly down the slope and continues to ski.

Fig 52   Aerial re-entry. Jumping off the bank the skier pivots in the air, often assisted by a pole plant, and re-enters the bank to continue skiing.

Jumps and Off-The-Lips

Little has been said about jumping until now as it is essentially the same, whether on one or two skis – except that to land on a mono demands a higher degree of control. Off-the-lips are an extension of the jump, the name being taken from the world of surfing. Look for steep banks where, with enough speed, you could get airborne and approach the lip at just the right speed to be able to stall. All that you then do is to perform a tail stall but with most of the ski clear of the bank. An extension of this idea is to approach at a higher speed and perform the manoeuvre in the air, known as an aerial re-entry.

These are just a few ideas to try; the rest is up to you, the terrain and your imagination. Whatever your ability and agility, I am sure there is an aspect of monoskiing that will open up new and exciting prospects, will take you into new terrain and add to your enjoyment of the total game we call skiing.

Appendix 1

Avalanche Awareness

The mono ski will allow you into what can be hazardous terrain, countryside, where the avalanche is a common occurrence and where skiers must try to understand as much about the medium on which they perform as possible. We all know the beauty of the snowflake, each one so unique that it almost defies classification, but classify we must, in order to communicate our ideas and knowledge. The International Commission on Snow and Ice uses a letter/number code to describe snow types. It has ten basic forms and is frequently supplemented by the Magano and Lee (1966) classification which has eighty categories. Clearly, as skiers we do not need such a complex understanding. We are concerned with the snow under and around our skis, how it gets there, how stable it is, and how to ski it. The following is a very simple classification which should be sufficient to meet these criteria. Some additional specialised forms will be added when I talk about the stability of the snowpack.

Light Crystals which when held in your hand can be blown away (classic powder).
Heavy This will not pass the above test and generally has a wetter feel to it (good snowball snow). Its extreme form is sometimes known as porridge!
Deep Higher than the ankle bone and sometimes, if you are lucky and a good story-teller, higher than the head bone! The term bottomless is used when there is apparently no base to the snow.
Shallow Between the ankle bone and the ground.
Crust Any crusty surface to the snow. Some-times it will break easily and consistently and at other times it will support your weight, giving way only occasionally.
Hardpack All those surfaces that will not allow the ski to sink in at all. Hard névé and ice are typical forms.
Softpack The edged ski will cut into this easily. This includes the beautiful and easily skied spring and corn snows.
Sastrugi Wind sculptured snow which is usually also hardpack.

Avalanches

Avalanches are probably the single biggest danger threatening the skier of real snow (this is a collective term I use to describe all the various types of snow that can be found off-piste). No matter how much knowledge you possess, the longer you spend in the high mountains the greater is the likelihood that you will be caught by one. A realistic appreciation of this aspect of the mountain environment is essential; avalanches can and frequently do kill. So, having issued this dire warning what can you, the skier, do on arrival at your chosen ski area to check the avalanche potential?

Firstly, check the previous weather. The greatest hazard is during and for about 24 hours after a new fall of snow. The pisteurs or ski-patrollers will frequently warn you of avalanche danger with signs or flags. You would be well advised to take heed of their advice as after all they do know the area. Immediately after and sometimes during a snow storm you will hear them blasting the slopes. They are using a variety of explosive devices in an effort to release any dangerous snow slopes. Generally they only clear those slopes that threaten the recognised ski areas. Unfortunately, we are often faced with an agonising decision: it has been snowing hard all night and then it dawns beautifully clear. Out on the slopes there is a metre of fresh new powder to tempt us. Is it safe? We can never be totally sure, but we can reduce the odds of making the wrong decision if we follow certain procedures.

Secondly, we should check out the local knowledge. Pisteurs, ski-instructors, Guides or even local skiers will know which slopes are avalanche-prone. They may not tell you where the best powder is to be found but they should not mind telling you which slopes to avoid. Some experts advise that slopes of a certain aspect are more likely to avalanche at certain times of the year than others, but I find this *carte-blanche* advice unreliable because there are so many other variables to take into account. Accordingly, I would prefer readers to evaluate each slope on its own merits at the particular time. Statistically, of course, these assumptions are correct, but how are you meant to know that your slope is not one of the ten per cent that will avalanche? To suggest that a south-facing slope is safer than a north-facing one, for example, is unwise, as this does not take into account the direction of the wind or the recent weather conditions, not to mention other more complex factors, you must consider as many of the indicators as possible.

Thirdly, on arrival at a prospective slope we can follow a number of checks:

1. Look at the surrounding slopes and if a slope of the same aspect, altitude and angle has avalanched, suspect yours and choose an alternative.
2. Look for signs of instability. Sun-balling and slumping can indicate a danger of loose snow avalanches. Cracks may be a sign of unstable slabs.
3. Dig a snowpit and examine the snowpack.
4. Use the ski pole test.
5. Test ski a 'safe' slope of the same aspect, altitude and angle. A safe slope is one which

is short, has an easy run out and where the consequences of an avalanche would not be serious.
6. Test ski the slope with the security of a rope.
7. If you are still worried and there is no alternative, choose the safest line.

I will explain these checks in more detail later, but before you can use them to evaluate the avalanche potential, an understanding of what triggers avalanches is necessary. I will try to keep the technical information to a minimum, as the references at the end of the book can be used if you have a special interest. We can divide avalanches into two major categories, loose snow and slab.

Loose Snow Avalanches

These are usually either innocuous looking sluffs, or the enormous powder avalanches about which we can do nothing. Sluffs can be dangerous when they are confined to narrow gullies, and a slope which shows evidence of sluffing should be treated with a great deal of caution. Similarly, a slope with signs of sun-balling should be treated with respect, as this also indicates instability.

If you do get caught in such a sluff, if you can retain your balance it is possible to ski out of it. I remember my first encounter with a small loose snow avalanche. It was a beautifully clear day and I was skiing alone in Thyon 2000 near Verbier. The slope had been beckoning me all day, but because it required a short scramble along a ridge to reach it, had remained un-skied. Being young, foolish and having little imagination I decided to investigate. On arrival at the slope I hung onto a rock and jumped up and down to test the snow; it seemed safe so I started. It was tremendous, the powder was even deeper than I had thought it would be – when I turned round to inspect my tracks I realised with horror why. There were no tracks to be seen anywhere, just a large

Fig 53   An avalanche has occurred here so we must also suspect the slope to the right. (*See* Fig 54)

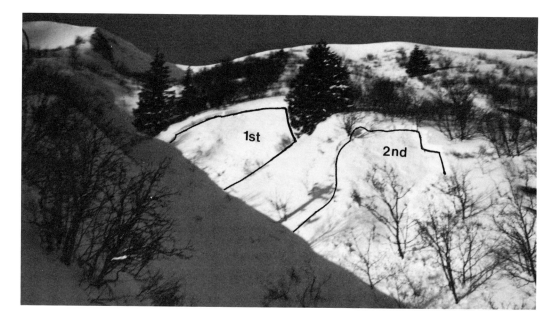

Fig 54   The slope to the right, which has the same angle, aspect and altitude, has now avalanched.

Fig 55   Cracks. This slope and those surrounding it are extremely suspect.

sluff. No wonder the powder had felt deep! I gingerly made my way back to the piste, a little shaken but much wiser. Even small sluffs can bury you; that lovely soft snow can pack like concrete when it comes to a halt. So, never be complacent about soft, light snows and never ski off-piste alone.

Slabs

Slab avalanches are a very different matter to loose snow avalanches; they are nearly always serious. There are several categories of slab but they all release in basically the same way. On another occasion in Thyon 2000, I was skiing with two friends. We had been skiing the same slope – good powder in the trees – all day, gradually working our way along a ridge. We chose a different line each time, and one run we decided on meant clambering down a few rocks. Clive went first, then me, closely followed by Tony. Clive moved on to the slope which

was quite compact, but as I joined him there was a loud ominous crump and a crack appeared right between my feet. Clive grabbed me, but not as quickly as I grabbed Tony who was still perched on the rocks. The slope did not go, but we did – back to the piste very chastened. Anyone who has experienced the sound of a large slab cracking will know what I mean when I say it is an awesome sound. You can feel the power that is about to be released. On that occasion we were lucky and I decided that it was high time that I learned more about avalanches.

What had probably happened was that the hot sun had been warming the rocks all day and these, in turn, had melted the snow lying next to them. This meltwater then trickled down beneath the snowpack, providing a layer of lubrication for the slab above to slide upon. This is the crux of evaluating the slab avalanche potential of a particular slope: there needs to be a layer of

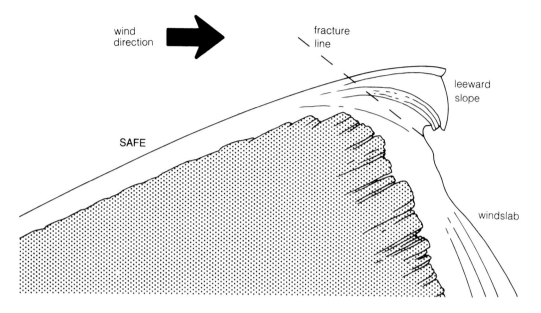

wind direction

fracture line

leeward slope

SAFE

windslab

Fig 56   A cornice with windslab below.

weakness within the snowpack. This weakness can take several forms. It can be a layer of water as described above or it can be a layer of ice or weaker snow crystals. A phenomenon known as depth hoar, which causes large fragile crystals or graupel, pellet-like crystals are typical layers of weakness.

Another classically unstable slab is windslab. As its name implies, it is formed by the wind. It does not have to be snowing, because the wind can pick up any loose crystals that are lying around. The number of crystals that the wind can carry depends upon its speed; the faster the wind, the more it can carry. It follows that when the wind speed drops it will shed some of its load, and this will consist of very broken up snowflakes because of all the battering they have received. These crystals will form into a firm cohesive slab which has little adhesiveness with the underlying layers or with any subsequent layers on top.

We can recognise windslab firstly by geographical location – it will only form in areas where the wind speed is forced to drop, such as on the lee side of ridges and in hollows – and secondly by its feel and appearance. It has a milky or chalky look and is usually smooth. Windslab will often make a squeaky noise if you plant your pole in it and then rotate the pole. A lot of sastrugi indicates that the wind has been blowing hard, as it is the wind which sculptures these shapes. These slopes, the windward ones, are safe, but watch out for the leeward ones where you will almost certainly find windslab.

The Snow Profile

The best way of assessing all these factors is to examine the snow profile using a snowpit. These can be dug using a snow shovel or the tail of your ski. It should be approximately 75cm wide, as deep as possible and on the slope you intend to ski. Smooth the sides carefully using the edge of the ski as this will enable you to see the structure more

Fig 59   Cut two oblique slots and prepare to stamp down across them.

Fig 57   A snow profile. Examining the layers.

Fig 60   Testing. By stamping down with my boot I have released a couple of layers which correspond to the layers of weakness. A very unstable layer will be released by a light stamp, or if you are using the shovel test a light pull. The ability to correlate the degree of force needed with level of instability will only come with experience, so dig lots of profiles.

Fig 58   A closer examination reveals several suspect layers.

Appendix 1

Fig 61   The shovel test. Do not lever the shovel but rather pull it perpendicularly.

Fig 62   A dangerous slab has been released.

clearly. Then examine the profile in a number of ways. First, using a bare finger (unless it is very cold when a gloved hand, ski pole tip or the base plate of a compass can be used) prod the snow every few centimetres (the weaknesses can be very thin). This will give you an idea of any hard or soft layers. You are looking for any marked inconsistencies; if it is to be safe, the profile should change gradually. Depth hoar will appear as a layer of larger than average crystals which feel glass-like, but which, with a little more pressure on them, will collapse spontaneously.

Secondly, examine all the crystals, looking

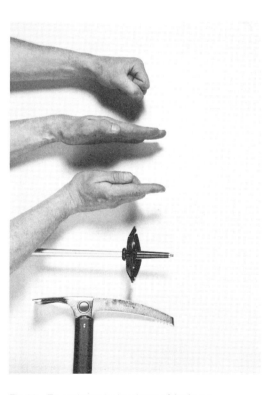

Fig 63   To evaluate the hardness of the layers more accurately you can grade the ease of penetration of the following: (i) fist; (ii) four fingers; (iii) one finger; (iv) end of ski pole; (v) end of the ice-axe pick. Be wary when low numbers are next to high numbers.

again for any marked changes in their size or texture.

Finally, look at the water content of the various layers. Free running water or very wet layers will act as lubricants for the snow above. If the pit reaches right down to the ground, examine that too. Grass or smooth rocks will obviously allow the snow above to slide more easily than, for example, a scree slope.

Having inspected the pit, there are two further checks you can make. Using the tail of the ski, cut two oblique channels down the back of the pit and then stamp down with your foot across these two channels. If a slab slides away then it is a good indication that the same will happen if you ski the slope. A similar check, which is probably better if you are carrying a snow shovel of the flat variety (the curved models, though good for digging, do not do this test very well), is to cut the same two channels as before and then to insert the shovel perpendicularly between the two cuts and to pull outwards horizontally, applying no leverage. If a slab is released by this action, you should suspect the slope. These slabs need to be at least 10 to 15cm thick to be of any concern; anything less can be skied with little trouble. If the snow is soft, you could ski a depth of as much as 20cm.

Digging pits every time you change slope can be very time-consuming, and a quicker though less informative method is to use the ski pole. Push the pole as far into the snow as possible; this may take several attempts. When you have a hole of some depth, move the pole in a circular fashion to create a conical hole which will allow you to check the profile. As you withdraw the pole, use the basket to feel for any layering in much the same way as you did with your finger. You can use this method to reaffirm information you have already gleaned from a snowpit. Another on-the-move indicator is to watch what happens to the snow beneath your ski, especially on a traverse: if it breaks in small (or big!) slabs, be cautious.

Fig 64   The ski pole test.

Test-Skiing a Safe Slope

The next procedure is to test-ski a safe slope of the same aspect, altitude and angle. Ideally you need a small slope where the consequences of a release will not harm either you or any other skiers in the area. You must try to stress the slope by skiing it vigorously. The reason for this is that just because a slope has supported one skier there is no guarantee that it will support others. This is a very important point, since as soon as a slope sports one set of tracks then everybody follows with abandon. Unfortunately, it is impossible to define how many tracks are needed to indicate whether a slope is safe or not, as every slope is different. Also, the temperature variations within the snowpack can cause its structure to change fairly quickly, so even slopes that have been skied should be checked.

Before you start test skiing slopes, I would suggest that you serve an apprenticeship under the watchful eye of either a qualified ski-instructor or a UIAGM approved Mountain Guide. The French insist that only people with the latter qualification should be allowed to teach away from the main ski areas, which are usually defined as those areas where there are glaciers. Do be careful when employing a 'ski guide'; some have neither of the above qualifications and just being a good skier is not enough. The judgement required for decisions made away from the piste demands considerable experience.

If you are in the middle of a day's skiing and are uncertain about a slope but have no alternative, then you could test-ski it with the protection of a rope to which you are belayed via a solid anchor. This, however, is beyond the scope of this book (*see 'Skiing Real Snow'* for advice on belaying and anchoring). What most of you will have to do in this case is to choose the safest line.

Choosing the Safest Line

It is very difficult to generalise as to which is the safest line, but these few guidelines may help. Fortunately, the easiest and most efficient route is often the safest. Stick to either shallow or very steep slopes as avalanches usually occur on slopes around 30 degrees (although they have been recorded on slopes of as little as 12 degrees). On slopes over 50 degrees the snow rarely adheres long enough to be a threat, but these slopes are too steep for most of us to adhere to as well! Wind-scoured ridges, although often unpleasant to ski, are usually safe. Tree-lined slopes are safer than open ones but avalanches can still occur on them. Choose slopes that have good run-outs on them and not ones which go over cliffs, into culs-de-sac or crevassed terrain.

If you have to traverse a dangerous slope, as leader you should choose an angle which necessitates using your poles to push you along. If you go any steeper, the people

wind

slab
avalanche

safe

dangerous

dangerous

dangerous

safe

Fig 65   A typical safe route. The wind will eddy around the ridges forming other
areas of instability. We must suspect all the slopes of the same angle, aspect and
altitude (these are indicated by the areas of shading). The safe route follows a
shelf, avoiding the valley which could channel any releases, and then continues
along a ridge instead of plunging back into the valleys.

behind you who are sliding on your packed tracks will be going too fast. It is important to cross the danger zone one at a time and when you reach safety to look back at your companions so that if the slope does go you can see where they disappeared.

In dire circumstances it would be wise to cover your nose and mouth with a Balaclava or scarf to prevent them becoming blocked by the snow. Many victims die from hypothermia so again, in very serious situations, ensure you are wearing extra clothing. The problem of whether to remove your ski under these conditions and walk is a very difficult one. On the one hand your ski will cut a ready-made fracture line, and on the other you may, by walking, cut a dangerously deep trough. The chances of skiing out of a slab avalanche are very slim indeed and it is more likely that your ski and poles will drag you further under. Certainly, remove your hands from the straps as this will enable you to cover your face if you get caught.

Emergency Procedures

If you get swept away by an avalanche what can you do to increase your chances of survival? Some you can ski out of, but in others, particularly the deep slabs, it would be very difficult. If you decide to try, use the techniques described earlier for skiing deep heavy snow, and at the same time keep looking for escape routes. However, only the very best and very cool skiers are likely to be able to cope, and even they would need a large element of luck. Alternatively, you should try to delay your departure by thrusting your poles into the substrata or leaping up the slope. Any tactic that will help you get near to the top of the avalanche is a good thing.

Once caught in an avalanche the best advice used to be to stay on the surface using a swimming action. Once, high in the Kulu Himalayas my partner was caught in a huge avalanche. He remained aware of his surroundings and by a rolling action not only managed to stay on the surface but also avoided being swept over some enormous ice cliffs. I have heard of several reports praising this rolling action; in fact, a Frenchman, for a price, has offered to demonstrate the technique! Any action that keeps you on

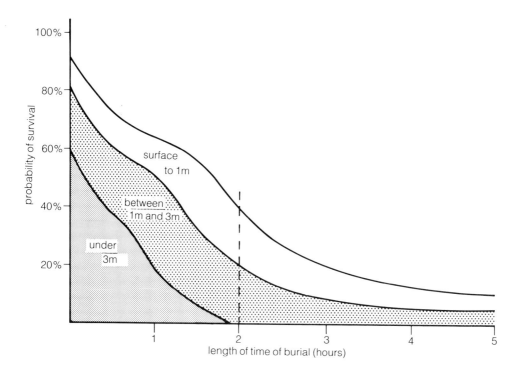

Fig 66   Survival time in an avalanche. The chances of survival diminish rapidly after a couple of hours, regardless of the depth of burial.

the surface is of value, but because of the conical shape of your body rolling also tends to move you to the edge of the avalanche. If you have time (and I have spoken to skiers recently who did) remove your sack, skis and poles as they will tend to drag you under. As the avalanche grinds to a halt make a last desperate effort to reach the surface. Anything that protrudes will aid your discovery by rescuers. As you become engulfed, cover your face and try to maintain a breathing space. Try not to panic and conserve your energy; shouting for help will probably be ineffective at this stage, although a loud cry as the snow starts to sweep you away may draw attention to you and allow would-be rescuers to see where you get buried. An analysis of Alpine avalanche statistics shows that after two hours of burial only twenty per cent of the victims survive.

Clearly, it is essential that any witnesses to an accident act swiftly. You will be shocked, but, although speed is vital, make sure that the slope is safe before commencing a search. If there are no further dangers proceed to the point where you last saw the victim and mark the spot with your ski pole. Your search should take on two phases; the first being a rapid search of the area looking for obvious signs like skis, clothing or poles. This search should take place no matter how close at hand the rescue services are. If, however, it draws a blank, and if, and *only* if, the rescue services are very close by should you leave the site and inform them. If they are some distance away, proceed with a more thorough search which should take the following form. Using the tail of your ski or your ski poles (you can get special poles that screw together for this purpose) probe the debris in an ordered pattern. With each probe site 70cm apart, work systematically over the whole area. As you can imagine this is not a very satisfactory solution, but by the time the rescue personnel arrive, the victim's chances of survival will have been reduced considerably. For this same reason the various devices on the market that aid

location by the rescue services are only really of value if the accident occurs within easy reach of them.

Party Precautions

The only satisfactory solution, besides not getting caught in the first place, is for each member of the party to carry a transceiver. This is a small device that emits a signal on a specific frequency; the two most commonly used are 457kHz and 2275kHz. The advantage of this device is that it can also receive a signal which is changed into an audio one that varies in intensity according to the proximity of the transmitter. There is one particular device being developed which uses a liquid crystal display to give a visual response. The sets are available in either single or dual frequencies and there is much debate as to which is the best. The International Commission for Alpine Rescue, IKAR, reports that the 457kHz frequency is significantly faster and more accurate. However, it will be some time before this frequency is adopted worldwide. The Austrians, for example, already have some quarter of a million sets of the 2275kHz variety in use, and the Americans report considerable interference on the 457kHz band from Trident submarines. I suggest that it would be wise to buy a dual frequency set.

When using a transceiver, follow the pattern illustrated in Figs 67 and 68. As the signal gets louder turn the setting down, because the ear can detect changes in volume more clearly at lower levels. With practice it is possible to search large areas quickly and thoroughly, but it does take practice.

If you decide to use transceivers, there are two golden rules to follow. The first is that they must be worn beneath substantial clothing so that they cannot become detached from your person. The second is that they must be switched on at the start of the day, checked to see that they are transmitting and then left on until you arrive

Using a Transceiver

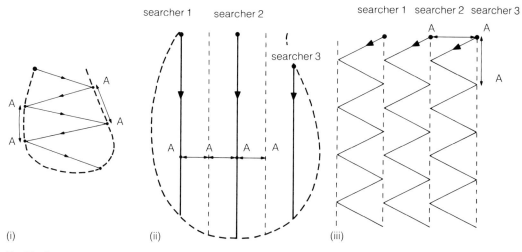

Fig 67 Search patterns. Distance AA must be within the range of the transceiver. Once a signal has been received, proceed with a fine search. If you are only looking for one person, turn the other devices off once a signal has been picked up.
(i) For one transceiver
(ii) For more than one transceiver
(iii) For searching a very large area

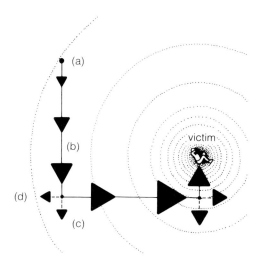

Fig 68 Fine searching.
(a) Orientate the transceiver to the strongest signal and walk in that direction.
(b) As the signal increases turn down the volume.
(c) Continue until the signal diminishes, turn 180 degrees and return to the point where the signal was strongest.
(d) Turn 90 degrees and if the signal diminishes after walking a short distance, turn 180 degrees and repeat the whole process until you can pinpoint the victim. This needs practice and you must stick to this procedure rigidly; do not be tempted to take short cuts, as it will usually take longer.

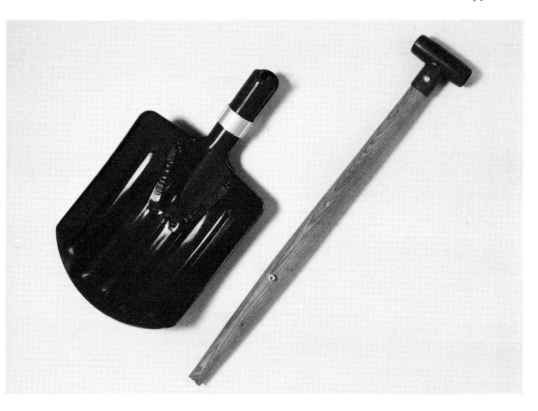

Fig 69   A snow shovel.

safely at your destination. Turning them on intermittently, only when you think you might need them, is just courting disaster. Some models have a battery check built into them, but for those that do not you will need to follow the manufacturer's recommendations regarding battery life. If in doubt, change them.

On location of the victim it will be necessary to dig them out as quickly as possible, and there is no question that a proper snow shovel is invaluable in these circumstances.

IKAR is testing a variety of other systems including a method developed by the Norwegians called *Suchwinkel* which uses dowsing rods and which, in spite of much scepticism, has achieved some very convincing results. Finally, IKAR has also been testing a gas-filled balloon which, when inflated, will lift you to the surface of the avalanche. Again, demonstrations have been impressive.

It would be unrealistic to ignore the information contained in this appendix. We all hope it will not happen to us, and with some of this knowledge we should be able to load the odds in our favour. I hope I have not put you off: awareness is half the battle in reducing hazards to an acceptable level.

Appendix 2

Learning Techniques

Learning new techniques and improving old ones is all about experimenting. All we, as instructors, can do is to give you guidelines between which you must explore all of the possibilities until you find what works best for you. Let us take edging the ski as an example. Because of all of the variables – the snow, the skis, the variation in body shapes, fitness and strengths – it is impossible to tell you the exact angle to edge the ski. You must learn it through experimentation. I often liken it to learning to drive a car or ride a bike. If you want to stop at the give-way sign at a road junction, your instructor will not be able to tell you to depress the brake pedal five centimetres in order to achieve the task. You will succeed at this only after a number of attempts. Many of the techniques in skiing are learned in the same way. Your instructor can give you the parameters within which to work so that you do not waste time and energy on inappropriate movements, but after that it is up to you. Only by varying your movements to the limits of these parameters will you really find out what works best for you and be able to apply the techniques skilfully.

When you watch a good skier floating effortlessly through the powder it is important to remember the miles that the skier has covered in order to reach that stage. Effortless it may appear, but in fact the skier is working hard and is probably also very fit. You cannot hope to improve dramatically with only one week's skiing a year. This was possible when you started but now that the tasks require a far greater awareness of the medium, there are no short-cuts. Imagine playing squash or tennis for only one week a year and expecting vast improvements to take place.

How can I, through the pages of a book, hope to help you when by my own admission miles and miles of skiing is so very important? The first way will be to offer you some of the guidelines, the parameters within which to work. Secondly, you need to understand a little about the way in which we process information so that you can help me to help you. The human brain receives information in a number of different ways, but we need only concern ourselves with three of them: visually, aurally and kinaesthetically. In other words, when you try to interpret the information your instructor gives you, some of you will respond better if they have demonstrated the manoeuvre, others to their verbal description and the rest of you to the sensations that your body received through its other sensory organs.

Good instructors will try to convey their message to their class through all three media. They will demonstrate, verbally describe the response wanted and ask for feedback about how certain things felt. You will probably find that one or other of these approaches helps you most. If you respond best to the demonstration then you are a visualiser, if to the words then your auditory system is the most dominant, and if you perform best by searching for specific sensations in your body then the kinaesthetic strategy is the one to adopt. Before you immediately say you are one or the other of these I would like you to test yourself. It is quite hard to establish with certainty which medium suits you best, but try this test. Try to remember a friend's telephone number. As you try to remember it, do you picture the sequence, do you say the numbers to yourself, or do you say them with a strong rhythm? If it is the first, your mind adopts a visual strategy to absorb information, the second indicates a dominant auditory system and the last a strong kinaesthetic sense. Establishing the relative role of your kinaesthetic awareness in the learning situation is difficult, but if you are the type of person who has always been quite good at sport, I would suspect that this is the medium your mind prefers to use to absorb information.

Now what has all of this to do with reading this book? In order to get the most out of the information contained in these pages you must establish which strategy you learn through and then convert the information into that medium. So if I describe a particular manoeuvre convert it into a sensation, mental picture, or a sequence of key words; whichever is appropriate. The text and the diagrams have been specially designed to help you do this.

As you work with the book, I want slowly to encourage your visual, and then your kinaesthetic, systems to develop. Those rare days when we perform perfectly, our minds seem uncluttered and our skis turn with ease are probably occasions on which these systems are functioning more effectively, and we can train ourselves to use them or at least to allow them to operate unhindered.

Visualising

One of the best ways of encouraging the use of these systems is *visualising*. A great many successful athletes from all sports use this technique to enhance their performance. Choose one of the techniques that you want to learn, read the text and look at the accompanying diagrams. The figures in the diagrams are deliberately without faces because I now want you to replace the figure with that of a friend or instructor whom you know can perform this type of turn. Imagine the friend doing these turns, linking one after the other, smoothly and efficiently, just the way you would like to be able to. Run this internal movie a number of times, then replace your friend's face and body with your own and watch yourself performing successfully. Run this movie several times and gradually try to feel your muscles tensing and relaxing through the manoeuvres, feel the cold air on your face, feel the changing pressures on the soles of your feet. Not only are you now seeing yourself performing the turns skilfully but you are feeling yourself doing them skilfully. Repeat this process the night before you go skiing and then just before you start your run. Be sure to make the mental movie as realistic as possible. This type of training needs to be worked at in just the same way as any other technique, but once mastered it should enhance your performance considerably.

Using Your Voice

We can also use our voices effectively in a number of ways. Most of you will have heard the grunts and groans of athletes when they are performing. These noises help to trigger responses from their bodies. Let us take a simple jump as an example. As you perform the movement say the word jump. If you say it softly and weakly then your jump will be correspondingly soft and weak; conversely, if your voice is explosive the jump will also be explosive. Our keywords need to be spoken in a manner that invokes the type of response we require.

Once you have overcome the embarrassment of talking aloud to yourself you should find this technique very useful. It also helps with the timing of the manoeuvre and with the timing of your breathing. The choice of word is important because certain words go well with exhalation and others with inhalation. 'Jump', or 'hop' for example, work well with inhalation, whereas 'sink' works with exhalation.

Fitness

I spoke earlier of the fitness of the top skiers and how important it is in order to realise your full skiing potential. People are generally more aware of their level of fitness nowadays, and there are many facilities and guidelines available to help you maintain a respectable degree of fitness. I will not expand upon training programmes here because this information is so readily available elsewhere, but I will stress its importance again. If you want to fulfil your potential, embark on a well-structured programme before you intend to go skiing.

Warming Up

One area that I will deal with in more depth is the process of warming up at the start of your day's skiing. I see so many people abusing their bodies in the name of warming up that I am not surprised by the number of injured and sore limbs and muscles that occur. It is very important to warm up on two counts. Firstly, if it is done correctly you will reduce the possibility of injuries and, secondly, it will enable your body to perform well early in the day. The success or failure of the first run often dictates the mood of the day, yet we rarely give that first run a fair chance.

Your warming up should ideally start back in the apartment after breakfast with a stretching programme that covers the whole of your body; this should then be repeated in a shorter form just before your first run. There are basically three different ways to stretch: statically, ballistically, and by a method known as PNF. Ballistically, swinging your limbs about, is the classic way we see people stretching, and it is a very dangerous way, although it is sometimes used by experienced athletes under the guidance of their coach to improve the integrity of the joints. I cannot overemphasise the importance of not stretching in this way, as you will do yourself more harm than good. Each time

the muscle you are working on is propelled to the limits of its range of movement (and more than likely beyond it) with this method, you will rupture some of the tissue, and the scar that results will restrict movement in the tissue. A shortening also occurs as a result of the reflex action that the muscle employs to protect itself.

PNF is a system that increases the range of movement by basically working the muscle against a static resistance at the limit of its range of movement and then stretching it. You should only attempt to use this method under supervision, as if it is done incorrectly, it could damage the muscles.

That leaves us with static stretching, which is a simple and safe system. You start by stretching until you feel a little tension in the muscle, but very definitely *no* pain. Hold this position for twenty seconds and then stretch a little further until you can feel tension again and hold that position for a further ten seconds, then that's it. I must stress the importance of feeling no pain; if you do, you are tearing the muscle fibres. You should repeat the programme at the end of your day's skiing as this is the best time of all to stretch, and it will help to eliminate much of the soreness that you may have felt on previous trips. Light exercise will also help by removing the waste products that have built up in the muscles during the day – a good excuse to go to the disco!

Once on the slope, I do a shortened version of the stretching programme, including some warm-up exercises like running on the spot. This is essential as warming up means just that. I then set off on the first run, taking it carefully, to allow my body to wake up and to feel what the conditions are like. I test my edges by doing fairly edgy turns, but not at any great speed, and I generally try to work my muscles thoroughly. At the end of the run my body is warmed up, but perhaps of even greater significance, my mind is confident that my body is performing well and that I am going to ski well that day.

Glossary

ABMG Association of British Mountain Guides.

Anchoring Securing yourself to the mountainside.

Angulation Usually used to refer to the way in which the hips are dropped to the inside of a turn (hip angulation) and to the medial movement of the knees as a fine tuning movement (knee angulation).

Anticipation A preparatory rotation of the upper body in the direction of the new turn.

Avalement A French term meaning swallowing. Very similar to compression turns.

Ballistic As in stretching. A bouncing stretch, to be avoided because of the very real possibility of damaging tendons and muscle fibres.

Banking Leaning to the centre of the turn.

BASI British Association of Ski Instructors.

Basket Usually a plastic ring on the bottom of the pole to prevent the pole from sinking in too far.

Belaying The action of controlling the rope so that a fall can be held.

Boiler plate A hard icy snow.

Button lift A type of ski lift also known as a poma.

Canting Methods which compensate for the variations in our leg angles.

Check A sudden edging action which provides a platform.

Compression turn A versatile method of turning that involves flexing the legs.

Cornice An overhanging crest of snow formed on the lee side of a ridge by the wind.

Corn snow Same as spring snow.

Crevasse A crack in the glacier caused by the ice flowing over a convex slope.

Crud Bad snow.

Crust A hard surface to the snow that will sometimes but not always support the skier (breakable).

Depth hoar Fragile crystals formed within the snowpack.

Drag A lift which pulls skiers up hill on their skis, or ski.

Edging Angling the ski so that the metal edge can bite into the snow.

Fall-line The line of greatest steepness.

Flow-line A line around which you feel yourself flow, more of a sensation than a clearly defined line.

Fracture line The line at which an avalanche has broken away.

Graupel Hailstone-like snow.

Guide A qualified mountain guide who has a UIAGM carnet.

Hard pack Hard icy snow.

Hypothermia A lowering of the core temperature of the body.

Imaging Another term for visualising.

Kick turn A way of changing direction whilst remaining in one spot.

Kinaesthetic Awareness of movement and motion.

Metamorphosis A process of change within the snowpack.

Mogul A bump of snow formed by the actions of skiers.

Off-piste Any ungroomed, unpatrolled slope.

Piste Prepared ski run or track.

Pisteur Ski patroller.

Poma Form of drag-lift.

Porridge Heavy wet snow.

Powder Light dry snow.

Real snow Snow untouched by piste machines and other skiers, natural snow.

Rime ice Ice that forms on the windward side of objects and indicates the direction of the wind.

Safety strap   A strap which joins your ski to your ankle so that you do not lose it in the powder.

Sastrugi   Wind-carved shapes in the snow.

Schussing   Running straight down.

Ski brake   A device that prevents runaway skis.

Slab   Snow which breaks into slabs.

Split fore-ski   A split in the front part of the ski.

Spring snow   Caused by constant freeze-thaw action.

Swallow tail   A V-slit in the tail of the ski.

Swing to the hill   The second part of a parallel turn.

Visualising   A mental technique that can enhance performance.

White-out   A condition where there is a mist and the snow blends with the sky leaving no discernible horizon.

Windslab   Slab caused by the wind depositing snow.

Bibliography

Avalanches

Barton, Bob, and Wright, Blythe, *A Chance in a Million* (S.M.T.).

Daffern, Tony, *Avalanche Safety for Skiers and Climbers* (Diadem).

Epp, Martin, and Lee, Stephen, *Avalanche Awareness* (Wild Side).

Fraser, Colin, *Avalanches and Snow Safety* (John Murray).

Symposium Report of the Alpine Club, Avalanche.

General Skiing

Abraham, Horst, *Skiing Right* (Johnson Books).

Howe, John, *Skiing Mechanics* (Poudre).

Hurn, Martyn, *Skiing Real Snow* (The Crowood Press).

Joubert, Georges, *An Art, A Technique* (Poudre).

Shedden, John, *Skiing* (The Crowood Press).

Shedden, John, *Skilful Skiing* (EP Publishing Limited).

Mountain Craft

Cliff, Peter, *Mountain Navigation* (D.E. Thompson).

Langmuir, E., *Mountain Craft and Leadership* (Cordee).

March, Bill, *Modern Snow and Ice Techniques* (Cicerone Press).

Pedgley, David, *Mountain Weather* (Cicerone Press).

Index

Index

Other Skiing Books from The Crowood Press

Skiing Real Snow
Martyn Hurn
1 85223 021 5

Skiing Real Snow shows you how to escape the crowded pistes and ski on fresh unexplored snow and, more importantly, how to do so safely. A comprehensive and practical handbook of off-piste skiing, it is essential reading both for those who already ski off-piste and for those who aspire to.

Skiing
John Shedden
0 946284 42 3

A step-by-step explanation of the fundamental building blocks of Alpine skiing, demonstrating each point with photographs and diagrams. Concentrating on positive, practical advice, John Shedden shows you how to improve your skiing and enhance your enjoyment of the sport.

Cross-Country Skiing
Paddy Field and Tim Walker
1 85223 070 3

With easy-to-follow instruction on basic and advanced techniques, and coverage of fitness training, equipment maintenance and safety, Paddy Field and Tim Walker explain the skills required for cross-country skiing, racing and biathlon. Fully illustrated with photographs and diagrams, this book will guide and inspire all cross-country skiers, whether recreational or competitive.